Practical Upholstery

COMFORTABLE FULLY UPHOLSTERED EASY CHAIR IN MODERN STYLE
The heaviness of many of the older upholstered chairs is avoided in most good quality work.

Practical Upholstery

C. Howes
Illustrated by S. C. Howes

Evans Brothers Limited London

Published by Evans Brothers Limited, Montague House,
Russell Square, London, W.C.1.

Made and printed in Great Britain by
William Clowes & Sons, Limited
London, Beccles and Colchester
237 44469 0   PRA 2825

CONTENTS

INTRODUCTION

ONE of the nicknames bestowed on the upholsterer by other sections of the furniture trade is " Ragtacker." I have been engaged in the rag-tacking business for a number of years and have tacked rags, or, to be more polite, fabrics on quite a varied selection of articles ranging from kiddies' chairs to motor gun-boats over 100 feet long.

The chief object of the upholsterer's craft, however, is to provide pieces of furniture comfortable to sit on and pleasant to look upon. It takes time and patience to achieve this object. Methods and designs are constantly changing and the good craftsman is always learning. During my early days at the bench I found it difficult to acquire sound knowledge and there were few books dealing with the subject. I hope, therefore, that this volume will help both those in the trade and home craftsmen to gain an insight into the craft.

Some of the items have been previously published in the WOOD-WORKER Magazine, and, since some of the materials and components that are readily at hand in a factory or workshop are not always available to the worker at home, alternative suggestions and methods are given.

I trust that all who are interested in the craft of upholstery will find some assistance in this book, and become worthy modern successors of the old-time craftsmen who took pride in turning out first-class work.

The drawings were contributed by my brother, S. C. Howes, to whom I am greatly indebted, and I offer my grateful thanks. I also wish to acknowledge the kind assistance given by firms in lending photographs of high grade upholstery showing workmanship that is worthy of the best traditions of the trade.

C. HOWES

CHAPTER I

HISTORY, TRADITION, PROSPECTS, ETC.

SINCE the days when our ancestors lived in caves mankind has continuously sought to improve his physical comfort. One of the earliest forms of a home was the tent, and it is probable that the craft of the upholsterer has evolved from that of the tent-makers of an early age. A worthy member of this ancient trade of tent-makers was that great traveller and apostle St. Paul. He is regarded as the patron saint of upholsterers. One of the oldest of the City of London guilds and livery companies is the Upholder's Company. It was granted a coat of arms consisting of a shield with three tents emblazoned in 1465. The Charter was granted in the year 1626.

At first upholsterers' work must have been mainly connected with wall hangings and bed draperies. Their earlier efforts at making chairs more comfortable seemed to consist of stretching strands of leather across the seats. During the fourteenth century the X-shaped chair made its appearance and it supported a cushioned seat. This was a big step forward, but upholstery as we know it at the present day, i.e. the stuffing of chairs, etc., did not become common practice until late in Queen Elizabeth's reign. Before that period both rich and poor had to be satisfied with the austerity of wooden seats. In fact, for many years after Elizabeth's reign it was only the wealthy who could afford the luxury of upholstered chairs.

From a few strands of leather stretched across the seat to the double- and triple-sprung easy chair, upholstery has passed through a variety of stages. Many anonymous craftsmen contributed in overcoming the difficulties and snags of their craft. Every little invention and minor improvement which has been handed down through generations of upholsterers has added something to the high degree of comfort of the modern easy chair or settee.

Historically the French and Italians are generally considered to have been the best craftsmen, but it is open to question whether British craftsmanship of the late Victorian and early Edwardian period with its production of fine buttoned work in moroccos, velvet, and damasks could be bettered.

Upholstery cannot be compared with engineering or any of the larger, highly mechanized industries. It is essentially a trade requiring patience, individual skill, and a certain artistic sense. Of

I

course, as in all the old handicraft trades, machinery and prefabrication are playing their part.   Ready-assembled spring units, hessian interlaced with stuffing, etc., take the place of much handwork. This is modern industrial progress which has its counterpart in almost every trade and, indeed, profession.   The carpenter has his doors and windows delivered at the site ready-assembled.   Even the doctor sometimes makes diagnosis on the results of outside laboratory analysis, whereas once he depended solely on his own skill.   This is progress and the clock cannot be turned back.   Many objectionable, monotonous, or tedious jobs can be done by machines with little human labour, and the general standards of living so improved.

One of the disadvantages is that the skill of the expert worker is often dispensed with and he loses that pride of craftsmanship which was a feature of the old-time craftsman.   A new entrant to a trade often learns only one section or process of that trade.   That is one reason for including in this book details of hand-sprung work.   This work, though gradually decreasing in volume, will for many years demand the use of these methods or modifications of them.

For the lad entering this trade the future is probably as good as in most trades.   There are still a number of small workshops left where a lad can gain an all-round knowledge of the trade.   Unfortunately these opportunities are decreasing as the larger factories are gaining ground and branded goods are becoming a regular feature of the retail shops.   However, whilst we remain individuals there should still be room for all who find pleasure and an artistic outlet in moulding fabrics, wood, and metal into comfortable and pleasant pieces of furniture.

CHAPTER II

TOOLS, NEEDLES, WORKSHOP REQUIREMENTS, MACHINERY

O NE of the minor blessings of the upholsterer's craft is that it does not require a large number of expensive tools. A quite modest outlay will buy everything required.

Most trades require tools for measuring, and upholstery is no exception. A two-foot boxwood rule and a five-foot linen tape are both necessary, and a six-foot flexible spring steel tape is often found useful. These can be bought cheaply, but it is advisable to consider quality before price whenever purchasing tools.

Hammers. Of the tools specially designed for the trade the hammer is probably the most important and the most used. It should certainly be of the best quality, and with an occasional renewal of the handle it will give a lifetime of service. There are two types—

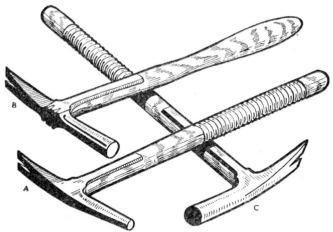

FIG. I. TYPES OF HAMMERS USED IN UPHOLSTERY.
A shows the cabriole hammer with small head. Both A and C have " ringed" handles, whilst B has pear-shaped handle.

one called a cabriole hammer, the other the tack hammer. The shape of both is similar, but the cabriole has a much smaller head, the actual driving surface being about $\frac{1}{4}$ inch in diameter, whilst the tack hammer averages about $\frac{5}{8}$ inch in diameter.

3

There is the choice of two types of handle, one termed "pear-shaped" and the other a ringed handle (see Fig. 1), the latter type being preferred by most upholsterers. In the past, when a great deal of show-wood upholstery was made, the cabriole hammer was extensively used. It is not needed so much with modern stuff-over jobs, but it is advisable to have one, as it is often useful not only for repair work and for occasional new work, but also for gimping, etc.

A more recent addition to the range of upholsterer's hammers is the magnetic head. The same shape head as the older pattern, it is split and magnetized so that tacks can be picked straight from the lips and driven home without using the fingers.

Scissors and knife. Next in the order of usefulness are the cutting tools. A good pair of scissors (Fig. 2) measuring about 9 inches over-all, fairly heavy but not cumbersome, is a necessity. Buy a pair with a reputable maker's name stamped on them, as nothing annoys so much as scissors which are constantly blunt, and which do not keep their edge when sharpened.

A knife for trimming off, particularly for hide and leather cloths,

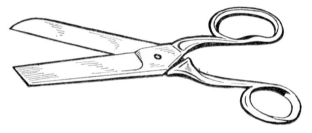

FIG. 2. STRONG SCISSORS, FAIRLY HEAVY WITHOUT BEING CUMBERSOME.

is also needed. Upholsterers seem to use all sorts of knives for this job—an ordinary pocket knife, a shoemaker's knife, an old lino knife cut down, or even a cut-down table knife. The kind of knife does not matter much so long as it has a sharp edge and point. The knife should be sharpened on a whetstone or an emery board so as to give the rough edge which is to be preferred to one of razor keenness.

Web strainers. Several types of web strainers are used, the simplest being just a plain piece of hardwood, shaped as shown at A in Fig. 3, and with a groove at one end. The web is brought over the plain top and under the grooved bottom end, as the strainer is held on the edge of the frame being webbed. It is gripped with the left hand and levered down until the strain is sufficient. A similar

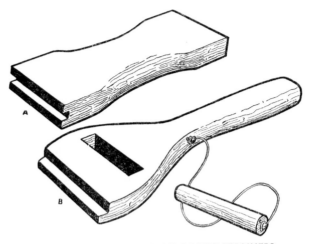

FIG. 3. ALTERNATIVE FORMS OF WEB STRAINERS.

A shows the plain hardwood kind in which the groove fits over the edge of the framework with the webbing beneath. B is the bat type. The looped web is inserted in the slot and the peg inserted in the loop.

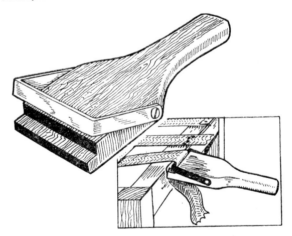

FIG. 4. LEVER-TYPE STRAINER WITH REBATED END.

The inset drawing shows how the web passes through the lever and beneath the end.

type has four or five spikes at one end, instead of being plain, but this is not much in favour as it is liable to damage the web.

Another design is shown at B, Fig. 3. With this type the web is folded and passed through the opening and the bar is inserted in the loop. The bottom end of the strainer is placed on the frame and

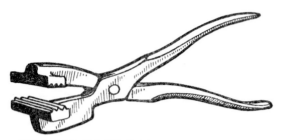

FIG. 5. WEB PINCERS WITH CORRUGATED JAWS.

These can be used for short ends, though long lengths can be gripped if the web is looped. In the case of polished wood the webbing should be passed beneath the projecting lower jaw so that the metal does not damage the wood.

FIG. 6. UPHOLSTERER'S RIPPING CHISEL.

Used to remove old tacks when re-upholstering.

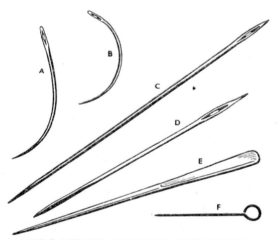

FIG. 7. NEEDLES, REGULATOR, AND SKEWERS.

A. SPRING NEEDLE.—Used for sewing springs to webs and hessians, etc.

B. HALF-CIRCULAR NEEDLE.—Used for sewing scrim and covers at awkward places.

C. MATTRESS OR STRAIGHT DOUBLE-POINTED NEEDLE.—For running-through the first stuffing.

D. BAYONET OR SPEAR-POINTED NEEDLE.—For stitching rolls or edges.

E. REGULATOR.—Used to regulate the stuffing.

F. UPHOLSTERER'S SKEWER.—Used for temporarily holding hessian, scrim, cover, and similar materials in place.

levered over until tight enough.   Many upholsterers prefer the lever-
type strainers.   The loose end of the webbing is passed through the
lever, and allowed to hang over the edge of the chair rail.   The
rebated foot of the strainer is placed upon the webbing and the handle
levered over, so pulling the webbing taut as in Fig. 4.   Another
straining tool is the web pincers (Fig. 5), more often called web
nippers.   These have corrugated jaws and are used on short ends of
web, but they often prove handy for pulling other materials tight.

The tools described above are all used in the making of upholstery,
but the ripping chisel (Fig. 6) and mallet are for the unmaking.   That
is, on repair work they are needed to remove the tacks from the frame.
The ripping chisel is held against the head of the tack and given a
sharp blow with the mallet, thus forcing the tack from the wood.
This should be done in the direction of the grain of the wood.

A medium, half-round rasp for rasping around facings, or where
an edge is about to be tacked, is also required.   Add a screw-driver
or two, a pair of pliers, a pair of pincers, a medium-sized joiner's
hammer, and a bradawl to complete the average upholsterer's kit
with the exception of needles.

Needles.   There are several of these, also some skewers and a
regulator (see Fig. 7).   The regulator is useful for many purposes,
the main use being to regulate the stuffing, particularly when stitching an edge to give shape to the upholstery.   Sizes vary from
8 in. to 12 in., 10 in. being the favourite.   The ordinary mattress
needle is made in various sizes up to 16 in. long and is double-
pointed with an eye at one end.   A 9 in. or 10 in. and a 14 in. will
be found to be the most useful.   This needle is circular in section
throughout its length, but its near relation, the bayonet or spear-
pointed needle, is triangular for approximately a third of its length.

A most useful member of the family is the half-circular needle,
which is also made in a number of sizes.   These are used in places
where it is difficult or impossible to work with a straight needle.

Last comes the spring needle, which, as its name implies, is used
mainly for sewing the springs to the webs and the hessian.   There
are a number of jobs, however, where it is very useful, places where a
straight needle is awkward and a circular one is not stout enough.
Upholsterer's skewers from 3 to 4 in. in length are used to hold
scrim, and coverings, etc., temporarily in position.

The main workshop necessities are a pair of stout trestles, and a
board on trestles or a table for cutting out materials.   The trestles
require wooden fillets all round the tops to keep the work in hand
from slipping off, as in Fig. 8.   A bag made of canvas or stout
mattress ticking with about four compartments is needed for the

various sizes of tacks. Add a white apron with a large pocket in front and you have the average upholsterer's working outfit.

The homeworker will not require many mechanical aids other than a good sewing machine with a piping foot attached.

For the trade generally many mechanized and power tools and machines are becoming available, including power sewing machines working at high speeds with many devices for piping and ruching and for closing cushion openings. Carding machines are not required so

FIG. 8. TRESTLES ON WHICH CHAIR FRAMES ARE STOOD
They are about 2 ft. 6 in. high by 3 ft. long. The wood fillets around
the top prevent work from falling off.

much now where fibre pads, foam sheet, and lintafelt have ousted traditional materials, but are still needed in repair shops. Electric cutting machines are used in factories, and electric shears are available. Cushion making machines for making spring interior cushions are less in use now with latex and polyether foams taking the place of spring cushions. Loose seat presses are used to hold the linters and cover in place whilst it is tacked or stapled round. Recently a number of stapling machines have come onto the market. At first the machines were filled with staples which were forced out by a trigger action. Compressed air systems have come to the fore on the larger units, and portable guns, electrically operated, are also available.

Air tools must be properly serviced, maintaining the correct air pressure and be well lubricated. All these tools are essentially for the larger workshops and factories. For the homeworker making single items the hand tools will be sufficient.

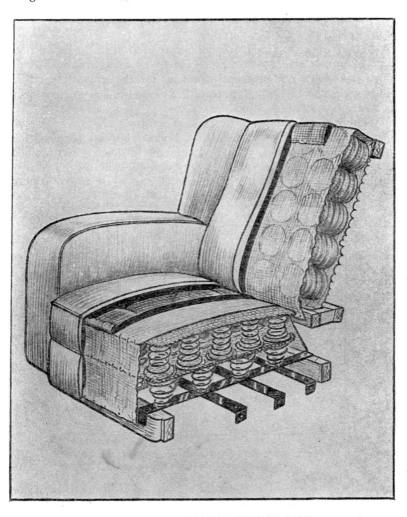

SECTIONAL VIEW THROUGH AN EASY CHAIR.
This shows the modern double-sprung unit resting on metal laths, the first stuffing, with roll at edge, and the second stuffing and final cover.

CHAPTER III

MATERIALS, STUFFINGS, SUNDRIES, ETC.

MANY different kinds of materials are utilized in the production of upholstered goods. Some are by-products from other industries, others are produced specially for the upholstery trade. They are garnered from all parts of the globe—in fact an easy chair is a very cosmopolitan affair.

Webbing. Beginning at the bottom, webbing still forms the base of a large amount of upholstery, though patent springing embodying its own base is a strong rival, and is largely displacing the webbed seat in new productions. Upholstery webbings are made in many qualities, the highest grade being a black and white twill weave of

FIG. I.   BALL OF TWINE AND ROLL OF WEBBING.
Webbing is usually put up in 18-yard rolls.

pure flax. Various other qualities of black and white web are made of mixtures of jute and cotton, or hemp, whilst sometimes linen threads are woven into the selvedges. It is generally 2 in. wide, but can be obtained $2\frac{1}{8}$ in. and $2\frac{1}{4}$ in. wide in certain qualities. All these varied grades of black and white web are commonly termed "English webbing" by the trade.

Plain brown or striped brown webbings are a cheaper grade, mainly all jute and of a plain weave. A large amount of it is produced in India and is obtainable in widths varying from 1¼ in. to 3 in.

Springs and springing play such an important part in upholstery that they are dealt with in a separate chapter.

Hessian. Next on the list are hessian and scrim. These two much-used materials are both manufactured from jute in many qualities, weights, and widths. The most favoured width for upholstery work is 72 in. The heaviest quality hessian, called "tarpaulin," is used on the best-class jobs as a covering over the springs, often termed "spring canvas." Scrim is a more open type of hessian and the threads used in its manufacture are rounded in section, whereas the hessian threads are flat. Its major use is for covering the first stuffing of fibre or hair which is afterwards stitched into shape, hence the term "scrim stuffing."

Stuffings. The principal stuffings used in present-day upholstery are fibre, hair, linsey wool, rugging, kapok, feathers, and latex rubber. Alva, a dried seaweed from the Baltic, was extensively used by the old-time upholsterer for the edges of the first stuffing. It was very easy to work when new, but became dusty and brittle with age. It was also affected by atmospheric conditions. Except when met with in an old repair job, it has quite faded away.

An old-timer which will be difficult to supersede is horsehair. Hair, as it is usually termed, is undoubtedly the finest and most resilient of stuffings, although as in most things there are numerous qualities. The cheapest varieties consist of short hair with little resilience. Quite a lot in use at present is reconditioned and contains a mixture of hoghair and hair other than that of the horse. Large quantities were imported from Russia and China, but lately most of it comes from America. It is washed and sterilized by various methods. After these processes it is twisted into rope, forming the curl which is retained throughout its life and supplying the resilience and springiness so essential. A large proportion is dyed black, whilst some is left its natural colour. These are called respectively black and grey hair, but the colour is not so important as the length and curl. The shorter the hair the less the curl, and therefore the less resilience and the greater the quantity required.

Occasionally dyed vegetable fibres are mixed with cheap-grade hair, making quite a useful mixture providing it is not sold as "all hair." The term "all hair" should only be used where the stuffing contains nothing but the animal fibre.

Coming to the vegetable fibres one of the most popular is coco fibre, often called "ginger" fibre because of its colour. It is the lining of the coconut husk and is prepared in several qualities. The best is a long fibre which has been curled similarly to hair, is usually free from dust, and is pleasant to work. The cheaper grades are not so long nor so clean, but make good stuffing for the cheaper class of work. The chief disadvantage of coco fibre is its tendency to break up and go to dust after years of use. It is also rather hard on the hands when being stitched into rolls.

Wood wool, shruff, or wood fibre, as it is variously termed, is a clean filling if new, and can be stitched into a good edge, but must be worked in very firmly. This makes for hard upholstery.

Another much-used fibre is termed Algerian fibre. It is the split leaves of a dwarf Algerian palm known as *crin d'Afrique*. Some is dyed black and some left in its natural green colouring. Hence the terms Black and Green fibre. The black seems to retain its curl better and it is softer and more resilient in use. The troublesome white mite has been found in the green fibre occasionally, so that most of it is treated by the importers to make it insect proof.

Sisal fibre was introduced into the trade shortly before the war and was chiefly used in spring interior mattresses and cushions. Another newcomer is a synthetic fibre made from one of the nylon group. This is claimed to be odourless, dustless, and non-brittle. It is white in colour and made its appearance before the war. It has not yet reappeared, so it is a little early yet to sum up its possibilities, although these appeared to be very good.

Stuffing pads. Hair, coco fibre, black fibre, and sisal are all being woven on to hessian by a needle point process, thus making ready-formed pads of stuffing. These pads can be obtained by the yard or cut to sizes. They are economical in use and are a useful addition to the large range of upholstery fillings. Other fairly recent additions to the list of fillings which have proved advantageous for certain jobs are rubberized hair, rubberized fibre, and the various forms of rubber cushioning.

Natural foamed latex rubber has been playing a large part as an upholstery filling and more recently the polyurethane foams have been introduced and will be also in much demand.

Flock, often called "black wool," sometimes linsey wool, has always been extensively used in upholstery. It is manufactured from rags and is the final stage of many a smart suite. The rags are washed and carded by machinery and rag flock must conform to the standards set up by the Rag Flocks Acts.

The felting process has been used with success on flock as on cotton, and felted flock or flock felt is much in demand. It is easier to place a layer of felt in position than "pick" loose stuffing evenly into place.   As with most forms of stuffing there are various qualities, these being graded by the wool percentage of the rags used.

A similar stuffing is called rugging, being produced from jute rags such as hessian and carpet backings, etc.   It does not possess the resilience of linsey wool and is more favoured for cheap mattresses than for upholstery.

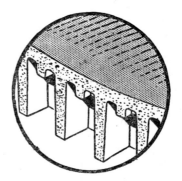

FIG. 2.   MOULDED LATEX RUBBER.
A section through a non-reversible latex
foam cushion.

Cotton flock, or white flock to give it the usual trade name, is a waste product from cotton.   At one time it was much used and the better qualities made good, clean filling.   The cheaper grades contain a large amount of husks and are heavy and lifeless.   A modern product from cotton waste is a form of felt made from linters.   This is an exceedingly useful production, being made up in several widths, thicknesses, and qualities.   Generally supplied in bales containing approximately 20 lb., it is taking the place of wadding over hair, fibre, etc.   It also makes an ideal stuffing over the springs of interior spring cushions and mattresses.

The list of fillings would be incomplete without mentioning feathers and kapok.   Both are used extensively for cushions and bedding.   The latter is a vegetable down from Java and the Dutch East Indies.   In this country its chief use is for cushions, although a number of mattresses are filled with it.   On the continent and in Australia it is popular as a mattress filling.   Quality is important with kapok, as with most things, the cheaper grades being dusty and not always pure kapok.

Feathers and down are graded in many qualities, the highest being real eiderdown.   This is plucked from the breasts of the eider duck. As only a very small quantity can be obtained from each duck and it all has to be plucked by hand, it is very expensive.

Most of the down and feathers used by the trade are duck and common poultry feathers.   The majority are imported from China and are washed and purified by the importers upon arrival. Cheaper grades of poultry feathers are often chopped or crushed to avoid the large quills being felt, but it does not improve the "life" of the feathers. This list includes most of the fillings in everyday use, but it is likely to be added to from time to time.

Feather cushions. When feather cushions are made up, the feathers must be contained in a feather-proof case. This is made from down-proof calico, and is a finely woven calico which has been waxed or treated to enable it to hold feathers and down.

Unbleached calico is sometimes used as a lining over the second stuffing before the final covering on good-class jobs, especially with hide work. In the past it was used much more frequently than at present, and it certainly helps a job to retain its shape. When the final stuffing is hair it is essential that a layer of wadding or linters felt is placed over the stuffing before covering. This is to prevent the hair working through the cover.

Wadding. Wadding is made in two forms: sheet or pound wadding. The sheet variety is put up in bundles containing 12 yards and the other in pound packets, as its name implies. Some upholsterers prefer the pound wadding, others the sheet.

Tacks. The ordinary blued, cut tack is the type most favoured. Various sizes are used for different materials, such as $\frac{5}{8}$-in. improved for webbing, $\frac{3}{8}$-in. and $\frac{1}{2}$-in. improved for hessian, and $\frac{3}{8}$-in. and $\frac{1}{2}$-in. fine for various covers. The improved tack is cut larger than the fine and has a bigger head.

The majority of workshops carry a stock of the following sizes: $\frac{3}{8}$-in. fine, $\frac{3}{8}$-in. improved, $\frac{1}{2}$-in. fine, $\frac{1}{2}$-in. improved, and $\frac{5}{8}$-in. improved; also $\frac{3}{8}$-in. and $\frac{1}{2}$-in. black cut gimp pins. One-inch steel clout nails or small wall nails are needed for patent springing.

Twines, etc. With the older methods of upholstery, twines and laid cord were essential sundries. A fairly thick twine is required for sewing the springs to the web, hence its name, spring twine. Another strong but finer twine is needed for various processes, such as stitching the rolls or edges, running through, etc. This is termed a stitching twine. Both spring and stitching twines are sold by the pound and generally put up in $\frac{1}{2}$ lb. balls.

Laid cord is a much stouter twine or cord, and the yarns are "laid" together in such a manner as to prevent stretching. It is used to lace or lash the tops of the springs in position. Twines are made from Dutch, Flemish, Irish, and Russian flax and Italian and other hemp. Quality depends not only on the yarn but also on the method of manufacture. A cheap twine may weigh heavier and thus give less yardage to the ball.

Much modern upholstery is finished with piped seams. These are made by inserting a piece of piping cord, covered with the material being used, between the two portions of cover about to be stitched together. There are several varieties of piping cord on the market, one type being a cotton cord of various sizes put up in hanks or on reels. Another is made of compressed paper fibre and is much firmer than the cotton variety. Both have their special uses.

Silk, worsted, and cotton cords, gimps, and ruchings are still used for finishing soft cover work, but not so extensively as in the past.

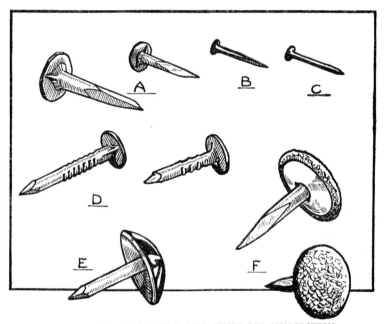

FIG. 3. TACKS, PINS, NAILS, AND STUDS FOR UPHOLSTERY.
A. Cut tacks in various sizes. B. Cut gimp pin. C. Wire gimp pin. D. Clout nails.
E. Round-head nail for finishing. F. Fabric or leather-covered stud also used for finishing.

Leathercloth and hide jobs are generally finished with studs and bandings to match, or with antique-coppered, round-headed nails. These round-headed nails are also made in bright brass, antique brass, and chromium-plated finish.

Foams, Latex, and Chemicals. Most crafts and trades have undergone many changes during the post-war period. The craft of the upholsterer is no exception. Tension springing used with a spring interior cushion started one big change before the war. This continued for a long period until challenged by the foamed latex cushion. Spring cushion units nicely made with pocketed springs and covered with a good linter's felt of sufficient thickness with possibly a thin layer of hair between them make a good seating unit. Badly made, insufficient filling, springs cockling over from the start and "feeling" through the cover after only a short period of use, have given spring cushions a bad name. Therefore the development of the foamed latex cushion was welcomed by the general public who were prepared to pay the higher price for, in the majority of cases, a more efficient cushion.

The chemist has changed not only the face of upholstery with new fabrics, but under the skin as well. Foamed latex rubber has brought many changes. At first only a few standard sizes of cushion units and mattress units were available. Any special sizes were quite an expensive job to produce. The position soon changed and now a large number of moulds of many sizes and shapes are available. Also "hand building" as it is termed, of special sizes and shapes is much less expensive.

After widespread use as cushions, mattresses, bar seat squabs, etc., many upholsterers started to experiment with its use in other directions. On arms, backs, and over spring units it has proved extremely useful. A piece of inch-thick cavity sheet cut to shape and held in place with an adhesive on the arm of a chair or settee makes a soft, comfortable arm with little labour involved. The same applies to backs and some seat units. Foamed rubber can be quickly cut to shape and joined with a rubber adhesive. It is not exactly a cheap material, but by eliminating labour costs it balances up fairly well with the older methods of upholstery. The combination of foamed rubber and rubber webbing offers the designer of upholstery the opportunity to create slim, slick productions.

An essential of this style of design is that the frame to be upholstered must almost fit the contours of the body before it is upholstered. In the older methods of upholstering spiral springs under soft layers of fibre and hair received the weight of the body, and supported it where the support was most needed. Where a slim design is made with foam the foam is rarely thick enough to give full support all round, therefore the frame must be "easy" to sit in before upholstering.

Another feature of its use, not noticed probably by inexperienced purchasers of upholstery, is the gradually decreasing sizes of the seats of the competitive type of fireside easies and settees. If they get much smaller they will be competing with the dining chair.

Designers with better intentions have made wide use of both cavity and solid latex in all its densities, sizes, and thicknesses. At the same time it seems as though even the best of them are inclined to sacrifice comfort for appearance by using too thin sections to give the slim line effect. Since the 1930's when foamed latex started to grow up, and since the war when it really did reach maturity, it has met no serious competitor until recently.

Chemical experiment and progress has resulted in the production of synthetic foam. The two most common are the polyether and polyester groups. Various advantages are claimed for both and they are considerably cheaper than foamed latex. A number of firms in this country and on the Continent, not to mention America, have been experimenting with these chemical formulae for quite a while and with a fair degree of success.

The better qualities are a useful addition to the list of fillings. They are being used extensively as cushion units as well as in arms, backs, and seats. Similar densities to foamed latex, light, medium, and heavy are made, and cut to various sizes as in the latex group; also made in cavity form and built up units.

An important difference between latex and the chemical foams is their resilience. The chemical foams are slower in regaining their shape. This laziness varies with the different productions, but the fact remains that it is cheaper than foamed latex and makes a reasonable substitute for cushion units of both spring and rubber. Perhaps it would be better to say it makes quite a good cushion, but is not so resilient as some other types at its present stage of development.

A feature common to both types of foams is the smooth nature of the finished product which allows it to be covered easily and cleanly. With the traditional methods of stuffing upholstery it was an acquired skill to be able to achieve a clean even surface by "picking" and "kneading" in loose fibre, flock, or hair. Therefore the chemical foams in the thin sheet form have become most popular in arms and backs, especially in the medium and lower price ranges of factory productions, and so the chemist controls the rate of progress and the methods of working in yet another old craft.

CHAPTER IV

SPRINGS AND SPRINGING

MODERN methods of springing vary considerably from the older hand-sprung method. Prefabrication tendencies have been in evidence for a considerable time in the upholstery trade. The upholsterer, particularly on new work as distinct from repairs, has much of his springing arrive as ready-built units. These units are formed by various combinations of springs, usually grouped under the term "patent spring."

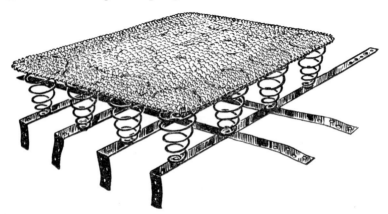

FIG. I. EXAMPLE OF A SINGLE-SPRUNG UNIT.

Spring units. For seat springing there are single-, double-, and triple-sprung units built up of coil springs; also combinations of pocketed springs on coil springs. Single-sprung units, consisting of a number of springs riveted to a base of steel laths, form the simplest type. The number of both springs and laths varies according to the size and quality of the unit. Some very cheap units suitable for small, competitive easy-chair seats consist of two laths crossing diagonally and having five springs set up upon them.

A better quality would have three laths each way and nine springs, one riveted at each crossing point. The top coils of the springs are woven into a lace wire mesh which holds them in position, thereby doing the same work as the laid cord in a hand-sprung job. This wire mesh covering also forms a good base for the stuffing to rest upon.

There are various methods, other than the wire mesh, used to keep the springs in position.   One consists of small strips of metal fastened to the top coils and passing from spring to spring in a similar manner to a laid cord lacing.   A wire frame surrounds the top of the unit, the outside edges of the top coils being attached to this frame with metal clips.   A variation of this method is the use of small horizontal springs instead of the flat metal strips.

Tendency to squeak.   Most of the methods used have something

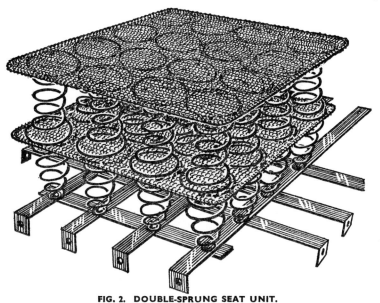

FIG. 2. DOUBLE-SPRUNG SEAT UNIT.
The bottom layer of springs is riveted to the crossing points of the steel laths.   The top coils the bottom springs and both the top and bottom coils of the top springs are interwoven into the wire mesh.

to recommend them other than mere cheapness.   At the same time they also have some disadvantages.   One of the most serious is the tendency to speak to you when sat upon, and not always in the quietest of tones.   This trouble is often met with even in the best of jobs.   Some makers have tried methods of insulating with varying degrees of success.   The wire mesh as a general rule does not give a lot of trouble of this nature.   There is often the chance, however, of the bottom coils hitting the metal laths and making a noise. This is usually overcome by pushing a piece of linters' felt or wadding between the bottom rungs and the laths.

Double-sprung unit. A popular form of double-sprung unit also has the steel laths for a base, with the bottom layer of springs riveted to the laths. A wire mesh holds the top coils of these springs in place, also taking the bottom coils of the top layer. The top coils of this layer are kept in position by a second piece of wire mesh. Most of the meshes are woven on a wire frame so that a firm edge is formed all round the unit. Slight variations of this type are often met with. Fig. 2 shows a double-sprung unit.

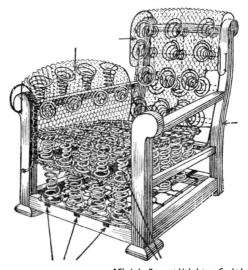

[*Chair by Buoyant Upholstery Co. Ltd.*

FIG. 3. EASY CHAIR FRAME WITH MESH TOP PATENT SPRINGING.

One method is to use strips of meshing about 2 in. wide, catching the outer top edges of two rows of springs each time and finishing on the wire frame. Before 1939 triple-sprung units made up as described above, but with three layers of springs instead of two, were occasionally used. These were more expensive and formed a luxurious seat.

A disadvantage with all this class of unit is the fact that the bottom layer of springs is almost always of the single-cone variety. This has a tendency to buckle more quickly than its double-cone brother. The top layer of springs takes most of the work, it is true, but the fact remains that with heavy wear the single-cone spring does become a cripple sooner than the double-cone type.

Yet another idea requires the laths to be fixed to the frame separately, the unit being placed upon them afterwards. The unit in this case is built up on a base consisting of a wire frame crossed each way with flat crinkled wire, each spring being interchecked at four points on its bottom coil—Fig. 3.

In a slightly different version the laths are fixed separately one way only, whilst the unit is built on a lath base, also with the laths extending beyond the springing one way only. These extended laths are fixed to the frame when the unit is finally placed into position.

One of the latest forms of springing which became popular before the war was the combination of coil springs and pocketed springs built on a base consisting of short horizontal springs and short pieces of steel laths or flat metal strips. This was termed a triple-sprung seat. A double-sprung version of the type omitted the top layer of pocketed springs. From back to front the short strips of lath are linked together by the short tension springs. These short strips are joined widthways by laths running the full width of the unit. Coil springs about 5 in. in height are fixed where the laths cross, and are covered and held in position at their tops by a wire mesh on a wire frame. A pocketed spring unit is laid on the mesh and attached to the wire frame. The better-quality units of this type have a flat steel tape sewn with wire, or clipped to the top edges of the spring of the pocketed unit, thus forming a firm surrounding edge.

Tension springs. Tension or cable springing, as it is often termed, has become popular. It is certainly a useful addition to the art of springing. This is particularly so when used in conjunction with spring interior cushions on the smaller chairs, etc. As the name implies, the spring wire is tightly wound in the form of a cable, $\frac{1}{2}$ or $\frac{3}{8}$ in. in diameter. Cable springs are fixed to the side rails of a chair by engaging a link or hook at each end over a nail, screw, or screw-eye; some manufacturers use a metal plate which is drilled to take the required number of springs and can be screwed to the frame. They are fixed at a tension of approximately to $1\frac{1}{2}$–2 in. on an 18-in. length. Tension springs are dealt with more fully in Chapter XXI, p. 160.

With the older methods, where a vertical coiled spring is involved, the action of the spring is to compress when it takes the weight of the body, while the tension spring, being slung or suspended across the frame, expands instead of contracting when in action. By using an interior spring cushion upon this hammock-like base a very comfortable seat is obtained.

Pocketed interiors. Pocketed sprung cushion interiors consist of springs encased in calico or hessian. In the calico variety each spring is sewn into a pocket of calico and then either steel clipped or tied with twine to its neighbours. The springs are of high-grade steel and average 3 in. in diameter, so that units can be made up any width or length in multiples of 3 in. The hessian variety contain similar springs, but the method of pocketing them varies. Some are termed wall sided, and have a wall or partition of hessian between each spring. Others have doubled hessian tops and bottoms cross-stitched in squares approximately the size of the tops of the springs. The inside pieces, both top and bottom, are slotted in each square to receive the top and bottom respectively of the spring.

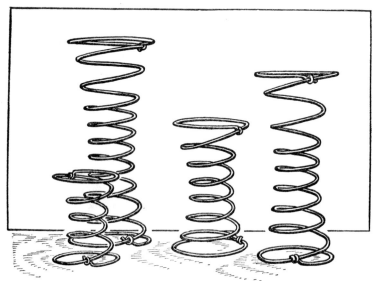

FIG. 4. EXAMPLES OF ORDINARY COIL SPRINGS.
These are the type used in hand-sprung work.

Yet another type of interior springing consists of springs interwoven one with the other so as to form an endless wire mesh of springing.

Coil springs. Before leaving this subject mention must be made of the ordinary common or garden variety of upholstery spring, which has stood the test of many years of service. It is a double cone, vertical coil spring obtainable in many sizes and gauges. The sizes most used and generally stocked are:

4 in. by 13 gauge   5 in. by 10 gauge and 12 gauge
6 in. by 10 gauge and 12 gauge   7 in. by 9 gauge
8 in. by 9 guage   9 in. by 8 gauge or 9 gauge
                                  10 in. by 8 gauge.

The smaller sizes and lighter gauges are used on backs and arms and the others for seats. The smaller the gauge number the stouter the wire. Fig. 4 shows some coil springs.

When deciding what size and gauge of spring to use much depends upon the quality of stuffing and the class of job. The majority of springs and spring units are made from copper-covered steel wire, but there is also a large quantity of black japanned and galvanized steel wire. Springs singly or as "made up" units probably form the most important single item making for comfort and durability of any upholstered article. Therefore, once again, quality counts.

A further addition to the various types of springing is the No-sag Zig-Zag and similar brands of springs built up on the circular arc principle. The wire is made in a serpentine strip then formed and tempered in a perfect circle. After being cut to the required size the spring is stretched and anchored between two points. This makes the permanent arc which gives it resiliency and strength. The springs are equally spaced on seats or backs and connected to each other with wire links. The two outside springs are connected to the side rails with $\frac{1}{2}$ in. diameter helical springs. Seats require heavier gauge wire than backs. An average back spring would be about 12 gauge, likewise a seat about $8\frac{1}{2}$ to 9 gauge.

One of the latest developments in this type of springing is the plastic covered spring. This can be used on cushion seats without being covered, as it has a clean, neat appearance.

A feature common to all these horizontal springs suspended between two points is that they help the designer to use more shallow surfaces. They also make for lightness which always pleases the housewife.

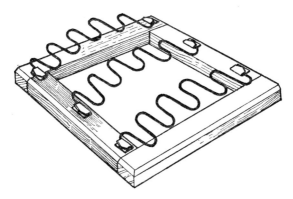

FIG. 5. METHOD OF FIXING THE SPRINGS MADE BY THE "NO-SAG" SPRING COMPANY.

206

FIG. I. FINE QUALITY REPRODUCTION CHAIR IN LATE 17th CENTURY STYLE.

An old chair of this period would have no springs, but these are added in the modern reproduction as they make the chair incomparably more comfortable.

CHAPTER V

FRAMES

UPHOLSTERED chairs and settees are built up on "frames."
This is the term used to describe the skeleton of wood or metal
which is the foundation for the upholstery. Until the post-war
shortage of timber brought about the development of metal frames
practically all stuff-over upholstery frames were constructed of
hardwood.

The post-war metal frame was either pressed steel or tubular

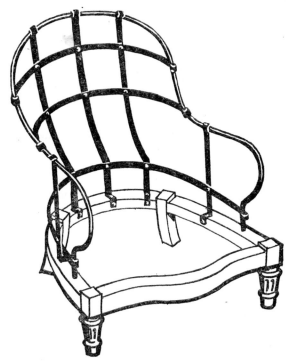

FIG. 2 THE OLD IRON BACK. NOW OBSOLETE.

A successful Victorian effort in comfort. This is a relic of the
days when an upholsterer needed more than a mouthful of
tacks and a hammer.

25

steel with riveted or welded joints.   Fillets of wood were nailed or screwed in position at various parts of the frame to receive the tacks of the upholstery.   If the frames were well made they would last a long time.   A disadvantage was that if the welding proved faulty most of the upholstery needed to be removed in order to carry out rewelding.

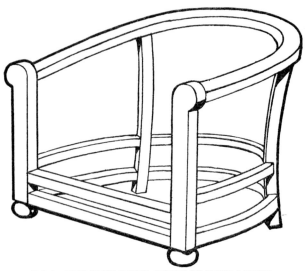

FIG. 3.   TUB EASY CHAIR, POPULAR WITH LADIES.
This is generally 2 ft. 1 in. by 2 ft. 1 in. and upwards in size.

The use of metal in frames is not new.   An early predecessor of the modern metal frame was the "iron-back" easy chair, one of the most comfortable types of upholstered easy chairs ever made (see Fig. 2).   The base, or seat frame, and legs were of hardwood, whilst an iron rod bent in a continuous sweep formed the outline of the back and arms.   This rod was held in place and supported by metal laths about an inch in width, these being bent over the rod and riveted at their crossing points, then screwed or nailed to the wood seat rails. This method of construction gave a springiness to the back which combined with a "fit your back" curve made for a high degree of comfort.

Wood frames.   To return to the majority of frames of timber construction, good, sound Quebec birch is the ideal.   Beech, oak, chestnut, ash, maple, and off-cuts of many other hardwoods are sometimes used.   Modern practice is to use dowels for most joints in frame making, though an antique or early Victorian frame may

have had mortise-and-tenon joints.   Properly glued and correctly
fitting dowels combined with carefully cut joints will make a good,
sound frame.   The main seat rails on large easies, settees, and other
big jobs require four dowels to each joint.   On smaller chairs, etc.,
three are sufficient.   Two dowels on the arm and back joints are
general, but each joint must be judged on its merits: whether the
rails are wide or narrow, and taking into account the stresses they
may have to bear.   Tacking rails are frequently fixed with a single

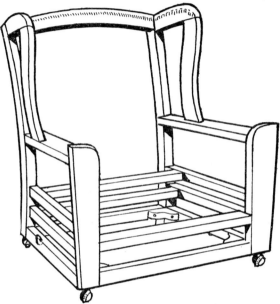

FIG. 4. WING EASY CHAIR, POPULAR AMONGST MEN.
Possibly a little old-fashioned, but still in demand.   A size of 2 ft. 4 in.
by 2 ft. 4 in. on the base is about right.   Fitted with Kenrick castors
for easy movement.

dowel at one end and housed into an upright at the other end, then
screwed or nailed.
    A frame should, to a large extent, conform to the general outline of
the finished upholstery.   One frame may, however, form the basis of
several designs by the addition of extension pieces and so on.   When
constructing a frame several points must be considered: height of
seat from the floor, height of arms, whether springs will be used on
the arms, is a spring edge to the seat required ? are double-sprung
units going to be used?
    Sizes.   The height of the seat from the ground should be in
proportion to the length of the seat from front to back.   Thus a
3—P.U.

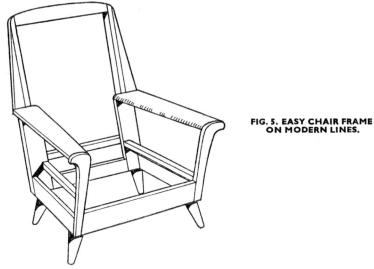

**FIG. 5. EASY CHAIR FRAME
ON MODERN LINES.**

A medium size would be 2 ft. 4 in. each way on the base for the chair.

**FIG. 6.   ANOTHER UP-TO-DATE
DESIGN SIMILAR TO FIG. 5.**

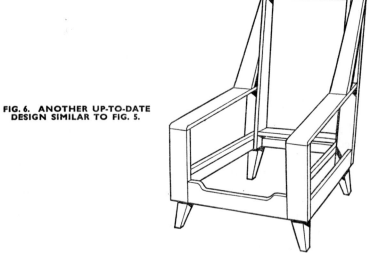

The variation is chiefly in the back, arms, and feet.

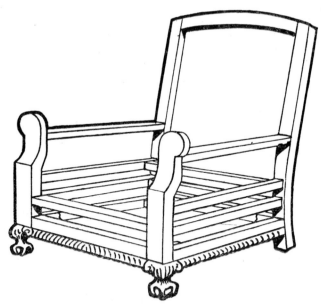

FIG. 7. SEMI-PERIOD TYPE TO HARMONIZE WITH OLD
FURNITURE.

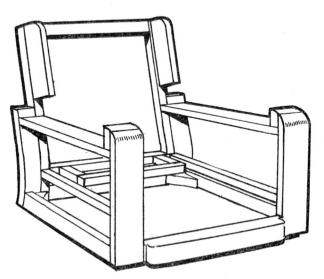

FIG. 8. FRAME SUITABLE FOR PATENT SPRUNG UPHOLSTERY.

large easy, intended for lounging and having a long seat, needs to be low, about 13–14 in. from the ground to the top of the front edge. A chair intended for upright sitting and having a short seat from front to back would be between 15 and 17 in. in height at the front. The arms and backs are likewise proportioned to the seat. If sprung arms are required the top arm rail must be set lower to allow for the height of the springs.

On a deep-sprung, webbed base, spring-edge job, double front rails and double tacking rails all round are preferable. A frame intended for a double-spring unit does not need the double tacking rails and according to the unit construction may not require two front rails. The bottom seat rails of a frame on which it is intended to fix a spring unit on a lath base can have $1\frac{1}{8}$-in. by 3-in. instead of $1\frac{3}{4}$-in. by 2-in. rails. There is not the same stress on these rails as when web is used. Corner blocks or braces are advisable on all frames.

Settee frames require a stout main front rail, especially the larger sizes. A centre stretcher rail is necessary on all the smaller settees and sometimes two are required on the larger types. Special springing systems may require additional rails, but the general construction is the same. Drop ends to the settee frames were popular up to the change in style from the scroll arm to the square-arm design. Since then they have almost faded out. Properly constructed they were very useful, although often a source of annoyance to the upholsterer, being awkward to get at and to finish cleanly.

At one time there were numerous metal actions available, many of them patented or registered ideas. In spite of this, variations of the wooden ratchet principle were much favoured, possibly because of cheapness and ease of manufacture through having the timber on the spot. Some of the metal actions were quite good and serviceable. One of the simplest was worked on the principle of a round rod passing through a hole at an angle. A metal plate with a hole slightly larger than the rod was screwed to a moveable wooden rail. As the rail was moved by a lever worked by the hand or foot (the lever projected through the outside cover) the rod passed through the hole in an upright position. When the lever was released a spring brought the rail over so that the edges of the hole gripped the rod at an angle, thus holding it rigid. Furniture design including upholstery has been at a standstill until recently. The combination of bent and laminated wood and plastic glues should provide some interesting types of frames on which to build upholstery that is both pleasing to the eye and comfortable to sit upon.

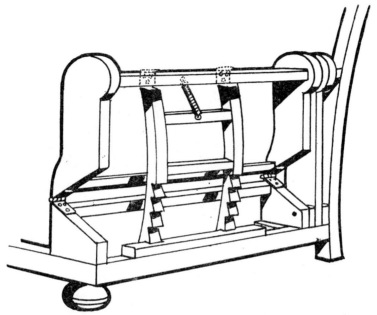

FIG. 9.   WOOD RATCHET TYPE OF DROP END.
There are several variations of the principle.

As the design of upholstered furniture changes so must the frame upon which it is built.   Wood still holds its own as a frame-making material.   Laminates of wood are used to some degree, but are generally more expensive and not so efficient at holding tacks as solid timber.   Tubular steel frames have had some success as some curves can be more easily obtained with steel, but the fixing of the upholstery is more difficult, sewing or adhesives being needed.

Moulded shapes of fibre glass supported on wooden underframes or on steel rods are being used, but are somewhat expensive.   All these variations of frame designs and materials help to make a variety which would be sadly missed in our homes if only two or three types were available.

COMFORTABLE EASY CHAIR ON PERIOD LINES.

Height is 36 in. over-all, width 31 in.   Height to seat cushion is 15½ in., depth of seat
cushion 20½ in. Width on front 23 in.

CHAPTER VI

GENERAL PRINCIPLES AND USEFUL HINTS

GENERALLY speaking, large upholstery jobs involve the same principles as small ones, and we give here some of the chief points to be noted when carrying out the various operations.

Webbing. Webbing forms the basis of most hand-sprung work. It must be tightly stretched across the space it covers. The strands are interchecked, thus supporting and being supported by each other and so ensuring maximum strength. In most cases webbing should

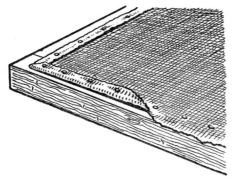

FIG. I. HOW TO TACK OFF HESSIAN.
Note how the edge is doubled over.

be tacked on with five tacks spaced as shown in the various illustrations in this book, three and two. These tacks are driven through the doubled-over web at the starting end. At the finishing end four tacks slightly staggered are used. These are driven through the single thickness of web and the web is trimmed off about 1 in. beyond them. This inch of spare web is turned back over the tacks and fastened down with two tacks.

Tacking methods. The tacking off or tacking down of various materials constitutes a large part of upholstery work. Web, hessian, and all materials that are likely to take a strain should be doubled over when tacking off. In this way the top layer of material acts as a buffer between the tack head and the second or main piece of fabric (see Fig. 1).

Where neatness alone is the objective the edges are doubled under

33

FIG. 2.   USEFUL FORM OF SLIP-KNOT.

as they do not take a heavy strain.   Examples are the cover on various parts of the job, hessian or calico bottoms, and the scrim covering of the first stuffing.   Hide and other real leathers are left raw-edged in many instances, as when finishing close up to show-wood or when the edge is covered with a banding.   Leathercloth can often be treated in the same manner, but not if the cotton backing is likely to show.

Twine work.   Sewing with various thicknesses of twine used in several types of needles enters into many operations in upholstery.   Thus knots and ties play an important part in the build-up of upholstery.   Most sewing operations are started with a slip-knot.   One of the most useful forms of this knot is shown in Fig. 2.   When sewing springs to the webbing start with a slip-knot, followed by the

FIG. 3.   SEWING TOP OF SPRING TO THE HESSIAN.
Half-hitches are generally used and a double-hitch when finishing.

simple half-hitch, shown in Figs. 3 and 4. The process is completed at the last point with a double hitch, and the twine is knotted before cutting off the surplus.

The same method is used when sewing the top coils of the springs to the spring hessian or canvas, as it is sometimes termed. Lacing

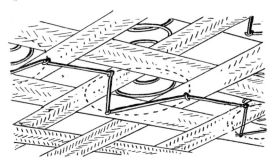

FIG. 4. UNDERSIDE OF WEBBED SEAT SHOWING METHOD OF SEWING SPRINGS TO WEBBING.

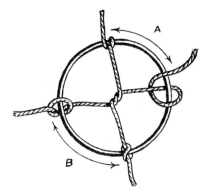

FIG. 5. ALTERNATIVE TIES FOR LACING SPRINGS,
A is the easier to regulate ; B the more secure.

or the lashing together of the top coils of the springs is done with a laid cord, a form of heavy twine specially made, or laid, to prevent stretching. Two methods of making the tie around the coil of the spring are in general use. One is a hitch, as shown in Fig. 5, *A*. By using this tie it is fairly simple to adjust the position of the spring if desired. The alternative method is a single knot, *B*. This is difficult to alter, but it is more secure.

Stitching the roll or edge is another operation started with a slip-knot. It is continued with a series of twists made round the needle. These pull into a tie as the needle is withdrawn (see Fig. 6). A single

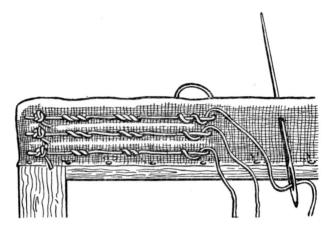

FIG. 6. STITCHING A ROLL OR EDGE.

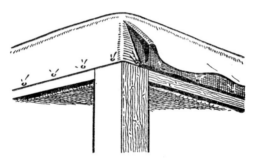

FIG. 7. SINGLE PLEAT FOR SQUARE CORNER.

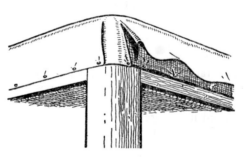

FIG. 8. ROUNDED CORNER WITH DOUBLE PLEAT.

twist is sufficient when making the sink, or blind stitch and for any intermediate stitching. The top or final stitch should always be pulled very tight, and by making a double twist the twine will remain taut as the stitching is continued. At the end of a row of stitching the final stitch is completed by knotting the twine before cutting it off. This stitching is dealt with in further detail on pages 58, 59, 82, 83.

Cutting materials. The usual method of keeping a straight line when cutting hessian or scrim is by withdrawing a thread. This leaves a wide space between the two adjoining threads which gives an easy mark to follow.

Calico and most cotton materials tear easily both ways, warp and weft. Leathercloths can be marked with a pencil and cut with the scissors. This is probably the safest way. Many of the cheaper grades of leathercloth tear easily, but they sometimes take the wrong turning and go off at right angles to the direction intended, so that care is necessary. Patterned materials can usually be cut by following the pattern through. In all difficult cases use a straight-edge and a piece of tailor's chalk.

Filling materials. Fibre or hair is the usual first or scrim stuffing; fibre generally because it is much cheaper than hair. These are used because they are easily stitched into shape to form a roll or edge that is both even and firm. Black flock or wool and hair are the top stuffings; wool because it is cheaper in price and does the job reasonably well; hair because it is resilient and retains the spring much longer than other natural stuffings. A layer of wadding or linters' felt is required over hair before the final cover, otherwise the hair will work through the covering.

Fixing tacks. Temporarily fixing covers, hessian, etc., in place with partly driven tacks is common custom. It enables the material to be gradually worked into position. Some operations in covering may need several fixings before they are finally tacked off, hence the need for only partly driven tacks. They can be easily lifted as the work proceeds.

Treatment of corners. Sometimes it is difficult to know the correct treatment for a corner. As a general rule a rounded corner needs a double pleat (Fig. 8), whilst a sharp or square corner requires a single pleat (Fig. 7). The main object with all corners is to keep the top part of the pleat or pleats below the top surface. Otherwise it gives an ugly finish, wears badly, and is poor workmanship.

Fitting the cover round show-wood arms, uprights, etc. There are often occasions when a cover must be cut to fit neatly to some polished wood. Turn the cover back away from the polished surface so the fold of the cover just touches the wood.   Mark with chalk or pencil a line from the outer edge of the cover to the point where the fold touches the wood and cut along this line.   Sometimes a double cut will be needed as on a fireside chair where the polished arms adjoin an upholstered back.   Practice is needed with most jobs, but these few tips should assist in keeping to the right lines.

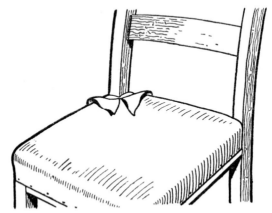

FIG. 9.   CUTTING COVER AROUND SHOW-WOOD SURFACE.

CHAPTER VII

PLANNING AND CUTTING COVERS

THE planning and cutting of the material for covering a chair or settee need care and forethought if they are to be done in an efficient and economical manner. The covering is usually the most expensive single item used in an upholstered article. Therefore the saving of a quarter or half yard of material is well worth while. Soft covers, such as moquette, tapestries, linens, damasks, etc., can often be joined in inconspicuous places and material saved. With coated fabrics, such as Arlinghide Lionide, Vynide, Florestin, and other brands joins must be avoided. The cutting of hides and morocco skins will be dealt with later.

Patterned material. Before bringing the scissors into action carefully consider the pattern (if any) of the material. If it is a large, centred design, such as a medallion, or a bunch or vase of flowers, it is necessary to centre the most prominent features of the pattern on the seats and inside backs. Stripes also call for special treatment; they must be either centred or balanced on the seat and back, and paired on the arms. If possible this should be carried out on the outside arms and outside backs as well. Sometimes this would mean too extravagant a use of covering material, but aim to work them as symmetrically as possible. In fact, whatever the design of the cover, whether large, small, striped, or all-over pattern, always strive for regularity of design, thus giving a pleasing finish to the work.

Joining. The object of a good cutter, then, is to lay out his material with as few joins and as little waste as possible. The joins should be matched unless they are going to be placed in a very inconspicuous position. Some materials present greater difficulties in sewing than others. A tapestry or damask will often join up with the seam hardly noticeable if the pattern is carefully matched, whilst a plain velvet or moquette never looks really well when joined.

The best method of sewing the last mentioned is by hand. Fold over $\frac{1}{2}$ in. on each side of the joining pieces, basting them down with long stitches. Butt the folded edges and sew so as to hide the stitches, leaving the basting stitches in until the cover is on the job.

Moquettes, velvets, and pile fabrics in general shade according to the direction of the pile. You can liken this to a cat's fur. If you brush it the wrong way it shows a different shade. This must

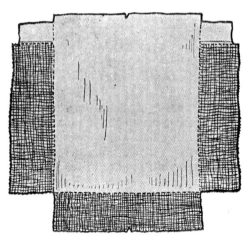

FIG. I.   SEAT COVER FLYED TO ECONOMIZE MATERIAL.
The fly is of less expensive but strong material and is used in concealed places.

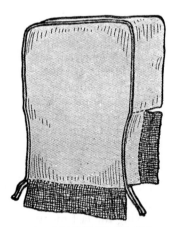

FIG. 2.   BACK COVER CUT TO FIT AROUND ARMS.
Note the flys.

always be remembered with these materials, and it is advisable to make certain of the direction of the pile before any cuts are made. A good plan is to mark the back of the whole roll or piece that is being used with a series of T's or arrows on each side of the centre line, i.e. on each half width.

Flys.   The term flys or flying up is used for the odd pieces of lining, casement cloth, hessian, or any odd cuttings which are sewn to the cover to save material where it is not seen (Fig. 1).   Thus the seat would be flyed on the three sides where it disappears under the arms and the back, likewise the inside arms and the inside back.

At the point where the arms merge into the back, the inside back cover is cut to fit over the arms and a collar or gusset-piece inserted and sewn as in Fig. 2.   This is often omitted on cheaper jobs, but makes a snug, neat finish.   With hide and leathercloth the gusset

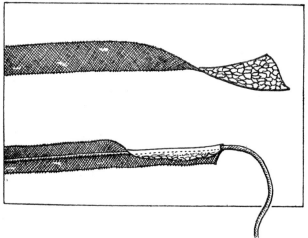

FIG. 3.   HOW PIPING IS MADE WITH INSERTED CORD.
The piping strips should be cut on the bias or cross whenever possible.

is essential in order to obtain a clean finish, and requires accurate cutting.   A piece of piping is inserted in most of these hard cover jobs, and, although this is not so frequently used on soft cover jobs, it is an improvement well worth the trouble.   Fig. 3 shows how the piping is made.

The terms used for the various pieces of cover are: seat, inside back, outside back, inside arm, outside arm, and front facings, the latter being the pieces of cover on the front of scroll or similar shaped arms.   Back facings are similar pieces on the sides of the back.   The front border is the front portion finishing the seat. Back borders are the finish to a square or shaped back, usually continuing from one arm to the other.

In the past furnishing cords and gimps were used to cover the finishing points of the facings and borders on soft cover jobs. Modern practice, however, favours the insertion of a piece of piping wherever possible. Leathercloths and hides are almost always finished with piping on all facings, etc., and most seams. Banding and material-covered studs to match or antique nails are generally used when finishing over a tacked-off edge.

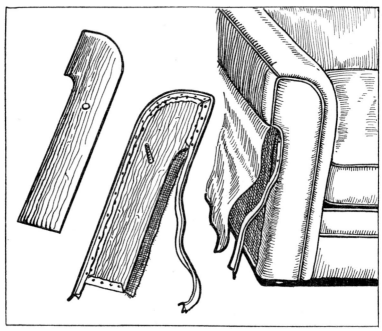

FIG. 4. HOW A WOOD FACING IS COVERED AND FITTED.
Note the bolt which passes through the front arm.

Facings. A neat finish to leathercloth or hide work is obtained by fitting wood facings covered with the material being used, as shown in Fig. 4. Make templates of stiff paper or cardboard and cut the required shapes from ply or other available wood. These facings are usually fixed into place with one or two bolts. Fix them temporarily with a nail or two, then bore through the facings and the frame. Countersink the hole to take the head of the bolt.

Remove the facing from the frame and insert the bolt in the facing if it is likely to be difficult to get at after covering. Cover the facing with a piece of the material, leaving the outside edge untacked. Tack a piece of piping all round, but leave it hanging loose on the outside edge.   Replace the facing on the job and bolt down tightly.   Next, tack the edge which has been left loose, also the piping, finishing off the outside arm or back up to the piping.   Another method is to use dowels instead of bolts, gluing and cramping tightly.

Cutting.   Now for the actual cutting of the material.   In most small workshops where nearly every job is different from the last the upholsterer usually cuts his own covers.   The measurements are taken with a tape measure when the chair has reached the first, or

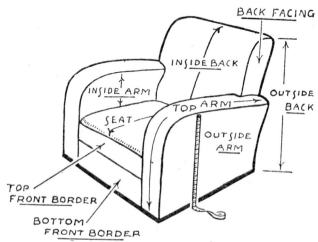

FIG. 5. METHOD OF MEASURING FOR THE COVER.
This shows the various sections and shows where the sizes are measured.

scrim, stuffing stage, or the calico stage if this is being used over the top stuffing.   Fig. 5 shows where the measurements are taken. Tuck the end of the tape between the seat and back just out of sight, and draw the remainder over the seat to the front edge of the point where the piping should finish.   Allow $\frac{3}{4}$–1 in. on this measurement for sewing.

On all materials that are closely woven and unlikely to unravel, $\frac{3}{8}$ in. is sufficient for joins and seams.   Loosely woven and thick pile fabrics require a full $\frac{1}{2}$ in., occasionally more.   Next measure over the inside back from the bottom to the top, allowing about 1 in. for sewing and tacking off.   Add a further 1–1$\frac{1}{2}$ in. to both these measurements for the top stuffing if measuring over the scrim.

The method of dealing with the width measurements is somewhat different.   In the majority of types of chairs a half width of 50-in.

4—P.U.

material will be sufficient for the seats. This also applies to quite a number of designs for inside backs. A full width will be needed on nearly all settee seats, inside and outside backs. In many cases the width alone of material will suffice for the settee seats, but rarely for the backs. This means joins, which should be equally spaced at each end whether a plain or patterned material is used.

The only exception to this rule is when using a small all-over patterned or plain material on a fluted or buttoned surface where the join can be hidden. It is best wherever possible to keep to the rule of joining at each end, thus equalizing the strain on the join as well as obtaining a balanced finish.

Arm measurements. The inside arms are also measured from the meeting-place of arms and seat. There are many shapes and types of arms and each must be treated according to type. A scroll arm is measured over to the underside of the top arm rail for the inside arm, and from there to the underside of the seat rail for the outside arm.

A modern arm as shown in Fig. 5 would require three measurements: one from the seat to the piping edge on the inside, another from the outside piping edge to the underside of the seat rail, and the third from the outside back edge of the arm over to the bottom of the facing.

The width measurements also call for discretion as to whether half or whole widths should be used. With scroll arms whole widths can often be planned to cover the inside arms, using the pieces left over for the joins on the front and outside backs of the settee, outside arms, facings, etc. For the outside arms the use of half widths with a join placed at the rear end of the arm is usually the most economical treatment for this type.

With the modern variety, however, the reverse often gives the best finish, that is, a half width with a join on the inside arm and a whole width on the outside. The outside back of an easy chair requires a half width, and the settee outside back a whole width with small joins. Most of the foregoing remarks apply to 50-in. or "double width" material. Single width material or 31-in., of course, involves more joins on the larger surfaces. Settee seats will require two and sometimes three widths, likewise the inside and outside backs. The same rule applies; make these joins away from the centre line. For instance, take a settee seat requiring two widths of 31-in. material. Spilt one width down the centre and join at the selvedges on each side of the remaining full width, carefully matching the pattern.

Cushions. The boxed border, feather-filled, foam-filled, or spring interior seat cushion is frequently used in present-day uphol-stery. Cutting the cover for these is not difficult. Make a tem-plate or pattern of stiff paper or cardboard if there are many curves to consider, and cut to that, allowing $\frac{3}{8}$–$\frac{1}{2}$ in. all round for turnings. If a fairly square or oblong cushion is required measure the space in the ordinary manner and add the sewing allowances.

The borders for a feather cushion can be cut about $4\frac{1}{4}$ in. in depth, thus finishing approximately $3\frac{1}{2}$ in. in depth. This makes a pleasing finish, neither too skimpy nor too fat for the average suite. With a spring-filled cushion the depth must be regulated according to the height of the springs used.

When making a cushion-seated settee or easy chair it is customary to use a lining or cheaper material on the platform seat. This is the portion of the seat 4, 5, or 6 in. from the front edge that is entirely covered by the cushions. On soft-covered jobs this saves about 4 ft. of 50-in. material on the suite. On hide and leathercloth jobs it is not only economical but necessary, since the cushions would otherwise slide about.

When making piping the material should be cut on the bias or on the cross, as it is more often termed—i.e. diagonally across the cover. This allows it to "give" or stretch when made up, thus setting better on the job.

Allowances must be made for the amount of fullness required when cutting for a buttoned or fluted job. It is better to err on the generous side in these cases, as nothing looks worse than a strained finish with this class of work.

The old proverb, look before you leap, can be translated into, think before you cut, and is sound advice.

CHAPTER VIII

HIDES AND MOROCCOS

HIDE or, as the layman usually calls it, "real leather" upholstery has been popular for many years. Hide is the shortened term used to classify cowhides. These are large skins covering an area of 45–60 or even more square feet. Moroccos are the smaller skins of goats. Roans are sheep-skins roughly the same size as the moroccos.

Amongst the old-timers in the peace and plenty era of the early part of this century morocco-covered upholstery was regarded as the highest grade of work. In these austere days moroccos are rarely used, but when they are they still require the highest degree of skill from the upholsterer.

Morocco skins are specially selected goats' skins, the best coming from the mountainous districts of Middle Europe, cheaper grades being from Persia, India, and other warmer countries. The goats live a very hardy life and have little fat or grease in their skins, hence their splendid wearing qualities. Thirty and even forty years in constant use is not a bad innings.

Moroccos often remain serviceable and retain much of their natural beauty for that period. Roans were used in conjunction with moroccos, the goat-skins being used on the fronts of the work in hand and the sheep-skins on the outsides. Roans have nothing like the durability of moroccos. Their place is generally taken by a piece of leathercloth in present-day practice. Cowhides gained in popularity soon after the 1914–18 war. The skins are cheaper per square foot than moroccos; also, being larger, they have a greater cutting area, thus giving less waste. They are durable, although not quite so long-lived in use as a morocco skin. Modern dyes and finishing methods have produced some fine, soft, and beautiful hides.

There are several grades and qualities, the two classes most used by the trade being termed full-grain hides and buffed hides. Buffed hides are those which have some defects and have been buffed over with carborundum. These are cheaper than the full-grained grade. Both grades, however, will give many years of service if not ill-treated—such as being placed too near the fire so the natural oil in the skin is dried up. Cowhides and moroccos are a different proposition to piece materials to lay out and cut.

FIRST QUALITY SUITE IN HIDE WITH VELVET CUSHIONS.

Planning out. The size of a hide is calculated in square feet and includes all the inlets and peninsulas. In fact, looking at a hide laid on the floor it can be likened to a map. The measurements include all the coastline. One of the methods of measuring is by a Turner pin-wheel machine, which registers every inch of hide. There is bound to be a certain amount of unavoidable waste. When measuring a chair or settee for hide, note where inches can be saved, such as at the two edges of the inside back, where the arms merge into the back, also on the inside arms at this point. Plan the positions of these pieces on the hide, marking out lightly with ordinary chalk. Keep a good look-out for objectionable blemishes, such as small holes made by the weevil fly, abrasions caused by injuries to the animal when alive or during the skinning and dressing processes. Some blemishes are not objectionable and occasionally add to the natural effects of the skin. A careful examination in a good light is necessary, as often innocent-looking marks turn out nasty eyesores when the hide is stretched over a job.

Handling moroccos. Avoid handling moroccos with damp or perspiring hands and carefully shade before cutting. There is often a slight variation in the shades of different skins. Another point to be noted when using morocco is that the markings along the backbone stand out fairly clear. These should be centred on the seats and backs, as when using a patterned material. All seams, borders, facings, etc., require a piped finish. This means accurate fittings on the actual job before cutting. Accurate fitting and cutting are vital if a clean finish is required, as leather cannot be manipulated like a soft cover and mistakes are not easily rectified.

Small joins and joins in obscure places can often be made by skiving one piece of hide to another. Lay one of the pieces to be joined on a flat board and with a very sharp knife make a long, slanting cut along the edge about to be joined. A thin knife well sharpened on an emery board makes a good clean cut. The other piece to be joined is cut on the reverse side to the first piece and the two pieces are glued together. Use a good flexible glue and after pressing together as tightly as possible wipe off any surplus glue. Lay aside on a flat surface until the glue is set. Short pieces of waste can be cut up for piping and made into one strip by this method. In fact, the old-time upholsterer used to join up quite large surfaces by skiving. The present trend of upholstery is mainly on clean, straight lines which do not call for much pleating or fulling in of material.

Occasionally one meets with a re-cover job of a different type. Rounded arms and backs, well-stuffed wings all mean that the hide or morocco must be neatly worked into pleats, or the fullness evenly spaced and distributed round a curved surface. Taking a scroll-shaped arm as an example, the hide is pulled over the scroll of the arm as tightly as possible and fixed temporarily in place on the underside. The spare material on the front of the facing is gradually worked into a number of evenly spaced folds. This is done by alternate straining and fixing with temporary tacks. Endeavour to keep the top surface clean of all rucks. If the folds are evenly distributed and tacked or sewn into place but not definitely pleated down flat, this usually makes a more pleasing finish. A thick piece of hide can sometimes be helped into place by damping the back, but don't overdo it so that it shows through on the surface.

Rolls, facing, etc. The rolls and edges need to be cleaner and a little firmer for hide covering. Front borders are one of the places where accurate cutting is necessary, particularly when the piping is under the roll or edge. Another place is on the back round the arms. Clean out all fullness when fitting before marking and cutting to shape. Where fullness has to be retained, such as on the fronts of scroll-shaped arms and over the edges of wings, it should be neatly and evenly spaced out. Each case must be treated individually, but as previously mentioned fullness worked out evenly in loose folds rather than in hard pleats folded down tightly looks better.

Whenever possible covered wood facings on this type of work are a neat and efficient finishing method. Studs and banding are occasionally used, but antique round-headed nails spaced about 1 in. apart and used both with and without banding are more in favour at present. Lead moulding, half-round in section with pins imbedded at intervals, covered with a piece of the morocco being used was one the recognized finishes on good-class work. The two edges of the strip of morocco were sewn together at the back of the moulding. When carefully tapped into position the covered moulding formed a neat and dignified finish.

CHAPTER IX

LOOSE SEATS AND PINCUSHION SEATS

THE ordinary dining-room chair having a loose drop-in seat, usually covered in leathercloth or hide, is familiar to most of us (Fig. 1). This method of fitting a seat has been in use for many years and is, if anything, more popular than ever at the present day. The loose seat, as its name implies, is made separately from the rest

FIG. I. CHAIR WITH LOOSE SEAT.
Sometimes the chair rails are rebated but in any case there should be clearance all round. This varies with the material, but ⅛ in. is about average.

FIG. 2. PLAN AND SECTION OF LOOSE SEAT.

of the chair frame. This makes for a clean finish, no gimp, banding, or other trimmings being required. It can also be easily removed for cleaning and re-upholstering.

Fig. 2 shows a plan and section of a seat. Birch or beech are the best woods to use for the frame, although quite a lot of the older frames were made of deal mortised and tenoned or halved together. Present-day practice is to use up any oddments of hardwood and dowel the joints, which is satisfactory if properly done.

Fitting the seat. Before starting to upholster make sure the seat is a good fit. Test it to see that it is true and does not ride on the corners. Then, having decided on your covering material, see that there is just sufficient space all round the seat frame to take the thickness of your cover. Too much space means an unsightly gap either all round or perhaps at one or two points only. This can be corrected by tacking a piece of cardboard along the loose side, or, if it is a very wide gap, a piece of web doubled or trebled over and tacked along will be better than the cardboard as it will give when placed in the chair.

Referring again to Fig. 2, note the position of the chamfer round the top. This should finish level with the top of the outside rails of the chair. If too high it results in an unsightly finish to the chair,

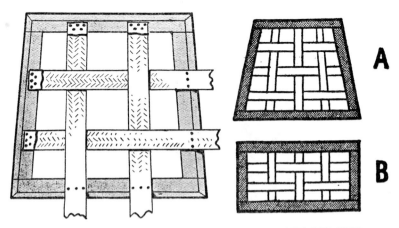

FIG. 3. ARRANGEMENT OF WEBS ON DIFFERENT SHAPES AND SIZES
OF SEATS.

and if too low it comes to the same thing, or involves a lot of trouble in getting the correct level with the stuffing.

Coming to the actual upholstering, hundreds, probably thousands, of these seats are turned out yearly by chair manufacturers, and all they consist of is the frame with a piece of plywood or fibreboard nailed on the top, and two thicknesses of linter's felt laid on and then covered. After being sat on a few times the linter's felt compresses and there is very little difference from sitting upon an ordinary wooden seat. Of course they do not wear out quickly, because there is nothing to wear, but the extra cost of webbing a seat is more than repaid by the comfort enjoyed.

Webbing. Decide upon the number of webs according to the size of the seat. A modern dining-chair loose seat measures approximately 16 in. by 14 in., and two webs each way as shown in Fig. 3 are sufficient. A larger seat requires three each way (Fig. 3A), whilst a dressing-table stool or other long, narrow seat three and two, as in Fig. 3B. Tack the centre web first whenever there is an odd number of webs being used, and equalize the others between that and the frame. Start to web from back to front, tacking on the top of the back rail with five tacks, doubling over the web, and staggering the tacks as shown.

Place the edge of the doubled part of the web along the top line of the chamfer. The web must now be tightly strained to the front, and this will be found awkward, as the seat will lift up as soon as the webbing is stretched. Fix the seat to the bench with a G cramp.

The method of using the bat type of web strainer is show in Fig. 4.

FIG. 4. USING WEB STRAINER.

The web is doubled and passed through the opening. A bar either of wood or a piece of $\frac{1}{2}$ in. tubing is put through the loop of web and the bottom end of the strainer is placed on the edge of the rail with the return end of the web under it and levered down. Do this several times until you have got the knack of it and can get the web tight and in the correct place. Tack off with three or four tacks. A $\frac{5}{8}$-in. improved tack is usually the best size for all webbing, but if you have a light frame use $\frac{1}{2}$-in. improved tacks. Cut off the web about 1 in. from the tacks, but do not turn over yet. Proceed with the other webs, checking the side ones under and over.

Hessian. A piece of hessian is now required about the size of the seat over-all. Fold over about $\frac{1}{2}$ in. of one side of this and tack it along the top of the back rail with $\frac{3}{8}$-in. or $\frac{1}{2}$-in. improved tacks. Slightly strain to the front and fix with three temporary tacks.

Repeat this operation at the side, keeping the threads of the hessian straight. When you have done this carry on with the tacking, stretching it as tightly as possible. Begin at the front centre and work all round, placing the tacks evenly. The raw edge can now be turned over, also the webbing raw edges with it, and tacked off.

Stuffing. If you have undone an old seat you may find a little stitched edge around the front and the two sides and a piece of wood nailed on the back rail to form an edge. On another type of seat a roll of straw evenly stranded and covered with scrim is used. Should the shaping of the chair be such that you cannot do without these edges or rolls, they must be replaced or new ones made, but there are not many of these types of seats in use at the present day.

The usual method is to stuff the top with wool or hair. Hair is the best and amply repays the extra cost involved. Place a few loops of twine along the top edges of the seat, using a bent needle (half

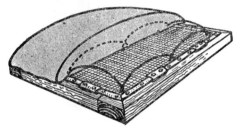

FIG. 5. SECTION THROUGH LOOSE SEAT.
This shows the hessian tacked off, loops of twine, and stuffing contour.

circular, spring, or packer's needle), just catching the edge of the hessian; also two loops across the centre. These are to prevent the stuffing from moving about and becoming irregular. Begin picking the hair or wool under the back loops and continue along the sides and front, finishing across the centre. Pick it out evenly, thin at the edges and coming to the thickest point on the crown of the seat, that is, slightly in front of the centre of the seat as in Fig. 5. The amount required varies according to the size of the seat and the quality of the stuffing; it should be firmly stuffed but not rammed in. An average seat takes rather less than 1 lb. of hair.

It is advisable to cover with calico before the final covering, particularly if hair stuffed. Lay a tape measure fairly tightly over the stuffing and allow an inch all round. Cut this size of calico, and fix it with three temporary tacks along the back edge. Pull it over the stuffing, pressing down lightly, and fix at each corner of the front edge. Place a tack or two temporarily in between. Do the same along the sides, and, starting from one side again, repeat the process until a nice even contour has been obtained. Finally tack off the sides first, then the front, and lastly the back. Do not turn in but tack the raw edge and trim off with scissors or a knife just above the bottom edge of the frame.

Final cover. The final cover can now be cut to size allowing $\frac{3}{4}$ in. to 1 in. all round. If a patterned cover centre the main feature of the pattern to the middle of the seat. Before starting to cover, if hair has been used, be sure to place a piece of wadding over the calico, otherwise the hair will come through. Place this wadding over the top of the seat only, allowing none to hang over the edge, otherwise the seat will not fit in the chair. First lay the cover over the seat

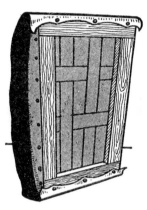

FIG. 6. WORKING POSITION
WHEN COVERING.
If held on edge it is easy to smooth
out the cover and tack beneath.

in the correct position, then turn the seat and cover over together, and place three temporary tacks at the back and also three at the front to hold the cover in place.

Until this stage all the work has been done with the seat flat on the board or table, but now the easiest plan is to work with the seat on its edge (Fig. 6). As the cover is tacked off on the underside place two or three fixing tacks along each side, straining the cover slightly as you proceed. After the cover is fixed on all sides start the final tacking off along one side about 2 in. from the front corner, and finish about the same from the back corner. Repeat along the other side, straining the cover slightly and helping it with a smoothing movement of the left hand. Proceed in the same manner with the front, then the back, leaving the corners until last.

When tacking off watch the cover to see that the pattern remains central and the threads of the material square. Leathercloth and hide have no pattern to worry about, but it is advisable to keep

leathercloth square.   Remember also to keep an even strain on the
cover from tack to tack so as to avoid ugly " cat's teeth," as they are
termed—that is, a little dip at each tack.

At the corner it is easiest to make a double pleat, as this lessens the
amount of material to get away at each side.   Pull the centre point
of the cover over tightly and tack.   Fold one side of the remaining
material and pull down as tightly and cleanly as possible.   On all
excepting the thinnest of covers it is best to cut a V-shaped piece out,
as shown in Fig. 7, but do not do this until you have formed the pleat,
tried it once or twice, and are quite sure of the position.   Some
loosely woven materials will pull out almost without pleats at all and

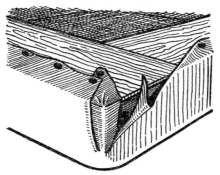

**FIG. 7.   FINISHING CORNER OF LOOSE
SEAT.**
The corner is drawn right over and a pleat formed
at each side.

the cheaper leathercloths are easy to work, but in the case of a very
heavy material it is sometimes advisable to chamfer a little piece off
the seat-frame before starting to upholster.   With the majority of
covers, though, due care and a tap with the hammer to flatten will
make a clean finish and a good fit.

When all the tacking off is finished trim off the waste cleanly.
Hide or leathercloth is best done with a sharp knife, and, providing it
is cleanly and evenly done, no bottom covering is necessary.
Tapestry, moquette, and other soft covers require a bottom cover
to present a neat finish.   Black linen, black hessian, calico, or hessian
are the usual materials used for bottoms.   Tack on neatly, turning
the edges under and spacing the tacks evenly.

The pincushion seat.   Before leaving the subject of the smaller
types of seats it is advisable to mention the pincushion seat (Fig. 8).
The whole treatment except that of the final cover is the same as for
a loose seat, only all the work is done on the chair itself.   There are

one or two points which must be watched.   There is usually only a narrow piece of frame left for the upholsterer to tack all his materials upon, so care must be taken when tacking that the wood is not split too much.   Use fine tacks with all materials and rest the frame on something solid when driving the larger sizes home.   If working on a polished frame place a piece of material under the web strainer to prevent scratching.   The raw edges must be turned in.

A bottom is not required on this type of seat, but a finishing trimming is necessary to cover the tacks around the edges.   On a soft

FIG. 8.   CHAIR WITH PINCUSHION SEAT.
The edges and tacks are concealed by the gimp.

cover this can be a gimp or a braid, though with leathercloth and hide a banding is customary.   The banding can be tacked on either with studs to match, or brass nails spaced evenly.

Some types of pincushion seat chairs look very well if the cover is finished "close nailed" with antique copper or brass nails.   For this tack off the cover first with $\frac{3}{8}$-in. gimp pins instead of tacks. This saves quite a lot of angry words as you will often find a tack head where you want to place a nail.

The secret of success with all the smaller types of seat having no springs and only one layer of stuffing is to use best English black and white web for the foundation and hair for stuffing.   The advent of moulded latex and polyether shapes for loose seats and other small jobs has simplified the stuffing of these small seats, but the same care is still needed to cover them neatly.

CHAPTER X

OPEN ARM FIRESIDE CHAIR

DURING the past decade vast changes have taken place in many trades and upholstery is no exception. New materials have been introduced and new methods of utilizing them have entered into many sections of the furniture world. The older methods of using loose hair, fibre, and flock, picking them in place under ties of twine, have been largely replaced by bonded materials. There is still scope for the specialist craftsman making individual items, but the large mass market is chiefly supplied by factory units using mass production methods. Their work has been made easier by the use of felted stuffings, rubberized hair, and foams both natural and chemical.

FIG. I. COMFORTABLE CHAIR WHICH CAN HAVE EITHER LOOSE OR TIGHT CUSHIONS.

Rubber latex foam is the natural foam and still the better all round product. Polyether and Polyester foams are chemical products and the chemists have made great progress with them. They have revolutionized the trade especially in the mass market section.

There are many grades and qualities, in fact at the time of writing *Dunlopillo* alone produce nine different grades, and there are other firms also producing large quantities. Rubberized hair, felted cotton linters, and felted flock are modernized versions of the older forms of loose stuffings. These all make easier and speedier methods of building up upholstery.

The spring-interior cushion, once largely used as the cushion unit in cheaper fireside chairs, has been almost completely replaced by polyether foam cushions.

Polyether foam is manufactured in sheets and can be cut to many shapes and sizes. This lends itself to building up interesting designs, such as the chair illustrated which inclines to the Scandinavian tradition. The show-wood parts should be of teak, that is, the arm sections. In practice the shaped top arm is often the only real teak piece, the remainder being beech or birch coloured to a teak finish. Another combination may be teak front upright or uphead, teak top arm, and the rest beech or birch. The covered parts are all beech.

Framework. Teak is not the easiest of timbers to fashion but when nicely cleaned up with scraper, finely sanded, and oiled with a teak oil it both feels good to the touch and looks good. Assemble the arms first, mortising and tenoning the front and back up heads; also the seat side rail. A single $\frac{1}{2}$-in. or $\frac{5}{8}$-in. short dowel can be used on the top of the up heads to take the top arm rail. Use a good glue and cramp tightly, taking care that the glue is a non-staining type. When the arm frames have set join together with the front seat supporting rail, the back rail, and the back support rail. Use three dowels in each of the seat rails, and two in the back rail. Fig. 3 shows the completed frame.

Seat and back framing, Fig. 4, can be made up separately using birch or beech. Two $\frac{3}{8}$-in. dowels are advisable for the back joints and three on the seat frame. These frames can be upholstered separately and screwed in afterwards. The under-seat rail which supports both back and seat frames can be placed in position and adjusted before dowelling so it will give the desired pitch to the back.

Upholstery. There are several ways of upholstering the frames. The seat can be tight covered or a loose cushion can be made up and the seat frame webbed and covered as a platform. The easiest method for the back is a tight cover. It is suggested that Pirelli or similar rubber webbing and foam are used for upholstering both seat

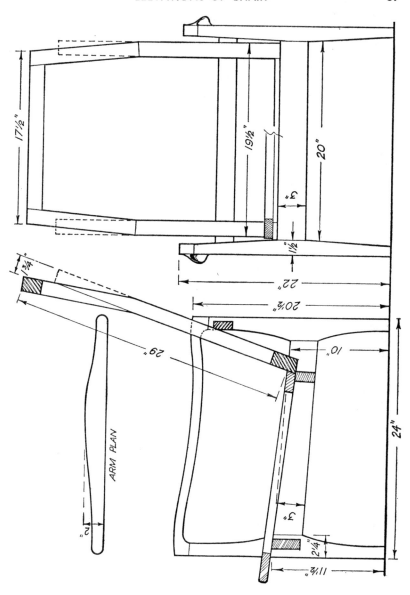

FIG. 2. SIDE SECTION AND FRONT ELEVATION.

and back.   Three-in. or 3½-in. foamed latex rubber is used on the
seat, preferably slightly crowned.   Take off the sharp edge of the
inside edges of both seat and back frames with a rasp before starting
to web.   Tack three webs back to front on the seat frame and two
crosswise.   If possible use a small clout nail ½-in. or ⅝-in. in preference to a ⅝-in. improved tack.   Allow about 1 in 10 stretch on both
seat and back using 2-in. web on the seat and 1-in. or 1½-in. on the
back.   Tack a piece of hessian over the webs on both back and seat
loosely, making pleats around the edges to allow play when sat upon.

The foamed latex unit for the seat can be of the non-reversible type
rounded at the two front corners.   It should be fixed to the seat
frame over the hessian.   One method is to stick a tape around the
bottom edge of the unit, either a piece of ready-made adhesive tape
or ordinary wide tape with rubber adhesive.   The lower edge of the
tape is left about ½-in. below the unit.   This edge is tacked around
the sides of the frame.   Another method is to stick the unit onto the
top of the frame with a rubber-based adhesive.   Cover the whole
seat and unit with light calico tacked on, raw edge on the underside of
the frame close to the edge.

A light, medium-density polyether foam is suggested for the back
filling over about five 1-in. wide rubber webs.   This must be held in
place similarly to the seat either with tape or adhesive, but calico is
not needed over the polyether.

Covering.   The next item is the covering.   Quite a number of
covering fabrics can be used on a chair of this type.   A fashionable
choice would probably be a plain woollen weave to tone with the teak
of the frame.   Measure over the tops of the two units from the bottom
of the back rails to the front edges of the units, plus ⅜ in. on each.
Cut these two pieces off and fit on to the unit tops to check, and round
the corners, keeping the ⅜-in. surplus all round for seaming.   Cut off
borders to fit round the front and two sides of both seat and back,
allowing the ⅜ in. for seaming and an extra inch on the back border
for tacking on the back rails.   Allow an extra 1½ in. on the seat
borders to turn under when tacking off.

Piped edges are avoided where possible over foam, as there is a
tendency for the edges to roll out of place.   A plain seam keeps in
place better and does not show so much if it does move a little.   After
machining the borders on to the two top pieces fix them in place on
their respective units.   Temporarily tack the seat cover on to the
underside of the frame, and the back cover also to the back of the
back unit.   Smooth out the covers and pull taut but not tight enough
to lose shape.

When working with the older forms of stuffing the cover must always be pulled tight enough to pull down the stuffing to a certain extent. With foams this is not needed, but the cover must be taut without being pulled down to any great extent as otherwise the clean line may be lost.

Tack off the back cover on the outside of the back rail raw edge. The seat cover is tacked off on the underside of the rails and is turned in when tacking down thus making a neat finish to the underside of

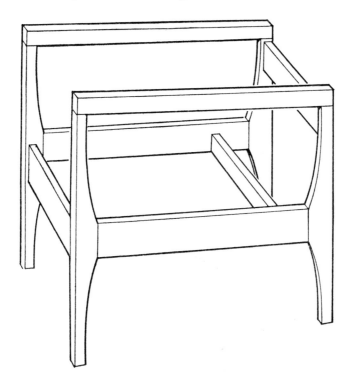

FIG. 3. HOW MAIN FRAME IS MADE.

the seat. It will not require a hessian or black linen bottom. The two units can now be fixed in place between the arms meeting on the support rail. Screw through the support rail from the underside into the seat back rail. Screw the back to the seat where they meet on the support rail. Also screw through the back upright into the arms at the point of crossing. A $\frac{1}{4}$-in. coach bolt or 14-gauge screw is needed.

The chair can now be completed with the outside back. This is back-tacked across the top back rail, stretched to the bottom rail, and fixed there with three or four temporary tacks.   The side edges are turned in and temporarily fixed down the back uprights.   Tack-off the bottom edge, finally on the underside of the seat support rail. Finish off the outside back by slip-stitching down the sides.

FIG. 4.   SEAT AND BACK FRAMES.

The neck or head pillow is just a small cushion made up of a light foam covered with the same fabric as the chair.   It is held in place with a strap made of its own material.   Fold a 5-in. wide piece of material in half and turn in the two edges.   Machine stitch along each edge.   Join into the cushion-case midway as that is sewn together. Cut through the strip halfway and join up again with a 3- or 4-in. piece of wide elastic.   This can be covered if a small sleeve is made up first and slipped over one end of the strip when cut.   It is slid down over the elastic when joined up.   This completes a chair that is comfortable in use and pleasing to look at.

ATTRACTIVE UP-TO-DATE SUITE IN TWO-TONE COLOURS WITH LOOSE CUSHIONS.

This is the Landore Suite made by Harris Lebus Limited.

STOOLS, SLIPPER BOX, KIDDY'S FIRESIDE CHAIR

THE sizes of stools vary considerably, the ordinary fireside type being about 17 in. by 11 in., height 12 in. A much larger member of the family is called a fender stool. It is about the same width and height, but much longer, usually 3 ft. to 3 ft. 2 in. over-all. Then there is the altogether higher stool for occasional use or for use with the dressing table.

FIRESIDE STOOL

Choose a type of leg which will match the furniture with which it is going to be used. The Jacobean twist in Fig. 1 looks well with hide or leathercloth covering. Having decided upon the size, prepare the seat rails. Birch or beech is suitable for the top seat rails,

FIG. I. THE JACOBEAN STYLE STOOL.

This has a light underframing of 1¼ in. by ¾ in. stuff. The seat rails, however, are heavier, being 1¾ in. by 1¼ in.

FIG. 2. STOOL OF THE 18th CENTURY.

This could be made in either mahogany or walnut. Note the attractive finish given by the piped border.

and these should finish $1\frac{3}{4}$ in. by $1\frac{1}{8}$ in. If the style of leg requires an underframe keep this as light as possible, about $1\frac{1}{8}$ in. by $\frac{3}{4}$ in. being quite heavy enough. It is advisable to mortise and tenon all joints. Glue and cramp, allowing the glue to set before fitting corner braces. Fix with glue and screws. When the frame is completed clean up with glass-paper and stain to the desired shade.

Webbing. Begin by stretching two webs each way across the top of the seat. Tack the webs on the top of the rails with $\frac{1}{2}$-in. improved or $\frac{5}{8}$-in. fine tacks. Fix the longest way first, doubling over the web when tacking on. Strain over tightly and tack off the raw edge, leaving an inch of web to be turned over later when the hessian has been fixed. Check the cross webs under and over, and strain and fix in the same way.

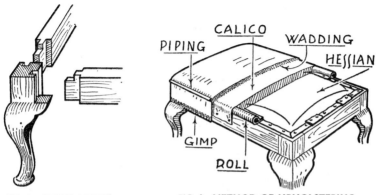

FIG. 3. FRAME JOINTS.   **FIG. 4. METHOD OF UPHOLSTERING.**

Place a piece of hessian over the webs, tacking this on with $\frac{3}{8}$-in. improved tacks, turning over the edges all round, not omitting the ends of web. A thin roll about the size of the little finger is made around the edges. Cut a 2-in. strip of hessian and tack this on to the top of the frame close to the outer edges. Put a little fibre on to this strip, then turn the hessian over and tack down so that a small roll or edge is formed all round. Make about six loops of twine around the top 2-in. inwards from the edge (Fig. 4).

Stuffing. A thin stuffing of wool, fibre, or hair is picked evenly under the twines. Cover this with a piece of calico, fixing on each side first with temporary tacks. Pull down and tack off evenly on the outside edges of the seat rails with $\frac{3}{8}$-in. fine tacks.

Cover. The next process is the final covering, and a modern finish is to make a piped border around the edge. Cut a piece of cover $\frac{1}{2}$ in. larger all round than the top, then four pieces for the borders. Lay the centre piece on the top of the seat and fix with a few skewers or large pins along the top edge of the roll. Trim this piece off to within $\frac{3}{8}$ in. of the pins, then fit the borders around the edges in the same manner and trim off. Make a few notches around the edges before removing both borders and centre piece from the stool. These notches are made for guidance when machining together.

A piece of piping long enough to go round the top is made up, and the centre piece and borders are machined together with the piping between. Stitch a plain seam without piping at each corner.

This method of making a piped border can be used with either a soft covering material or hide and leathercloth. Place a piece of wadding over the calico before laying the cover upon the seat. Temporarily tack the cover along each side until it is evenly strained all over, finally tacking off on the underside of the seat rail, turning in, and spacing the tacks evenly. Tack around the legs at each corner raw edge, and trim off with a sharp knife.

Finish with a gimp on soft covers, studs, or antique nails and banding on hide, etc. The gimp can very often be glued or pasted where a thin material is used. Otherwise use $\frac{3}{8}$-in. gimp pins and hide the heads under the scrolls of the gimp. It is advisable to complete the polishing of the legs before gimping.

DRESSING-TABLE STOOL

A stool of this kind is useful in both bedroom and living-room.

Framework. The legs should be in good hardwood. They are tapered from $1\frac{1}{4}$ in. square at the top to 1 in. or $\frac{7}{8}$ in. at the bottom. Any odd pieces of hardwood can be utilized for the side rails. They finish $1\frac{7}{8}$ in. by 1 in. and are tenoned into the legs. The two end stretcher rails are tenoned to the legs and the centre stretcher rail dovetailed from the underside. Glue and cramp up and fit blocks or braces in the corners. These are necessary for strength and should be well fitted before gluing and screwing. Do not commence to upholster until the glue has thoroughly set.

Webbing. Webbing is the first item and it is advisable to use $\frac{1}{2}$-in. clout nails for this. Tacks, especially the $\frac{5}{8}$-in. improved variety usually used for webbing, are liable to split narrow rails. Strain the webs on tightly, the short ones first, and check the long ones under and over as in Fig. 6. Cut a piece of hessian the required size, that is about 1 in. larger all round than the top of the stool. Strain this on tightly, doubling over the raw edges and using $\frac{3}{8}$-in. or $\frac{1}{2}$-in. improved tacks.

A thin roll is necessary on the edges of the seat to relieve the sharpness of the woodwork. This can be formed by tacking a $1\frac{1}{2}$-in. strip of hessian all round the top edges of the rails as near the fronts as possible. Lay a little wool or fibre on to this strip and turn the hessian over the stuffing to form a small roll of about $\frac{1}{4}$ in.

FIG. 5. SUITABLE FOR BEDROOM OR LIVING-ROOM.

Note the attractive finish given at the edges. Height is 17 in. to the framework. Seat size is 18 in. by 12 in. For the living-room the height could be cut down somewhat.

diameter (Fig. 7). Alternatively, a thick piece of packing cord can be used instead of the stuffing to form this edge.

Stuffing. The seat is now ready for the main stuffing, which may be either wool or hair. Take about 2 yards of twine and run a series of long loops around the hessian about 2 in. inwards from the front edges of the stool. Starting from one corner, place small quantities of stuffing under these loops, picking it out evenly. Fill in the centre, merging the whole so that a thin, even layer of stuffing is obtained.

If hair is being used it is advisable to cover with calico before the final covering. A piece of wadding or lintafelt should also be placed over the calico to prevent the hair pricking through. These items are not necessary with wool, the cover going immediately over the stuffing.

Covering. Odd pieces of tapestry, damask, linen, moquette,

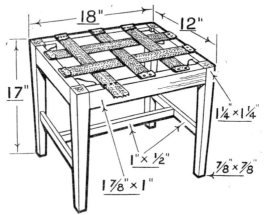

FIG. 6. FRAMEWORK SIZES AND WEBBING DETAILS.

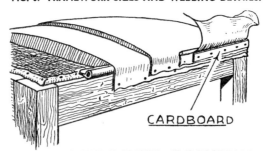

CARDBOARD

FIG. 7. HOW EDGING IS FORMED. IT IS BACK-TACKED.

or velour are equally suitable for covering. A pleasant effect can be obtained by using a piece of needlework for the top and bordering it with face cloth or a felted cloth of similar type. Lay the centre piece of cover on the seat and fix all round with temporary tacks, gently straining into place as proceeding. Make sure the pattern (if any) is centred and then tack off with ⅜-in. fine tacks along the front edges of the rails. Cut the four border pieces about 1 in. wider than the rails, also some strips for piping. Join the borders together at *three* corners and machine the piping along the top edge of the border. Place the border wrong side outwards and with the piping as near the top of the woodwork as possible. Temporarily tack in this position and then lay a ½-in. strip of cardboard along the hem of the piping and tack off through this cardboard.

It is usual to tuck a thin layer of wadding under the border just sufficient to give a soft effect. The bottom edges of the border are tacked off on the undersides of the rails and the fourth corner seam is neatly sewn. A piece of gimp pinned around the bottom edge gives a smart finish.

SLIPPER BOX

This is a useful article, serving the dual purposes of an extra seat and a hiding-place for slippers, magazines, etc. It can be made to practically any reasonable size in length and breadth, but the height from the floor should not exceed 14 in.

The box. Take as an example the following dimensions, 19 in. by 14 in. wide, total height over all 12 in. The first item is to make the box, using ¾-in. deal 8 in. wide for the sides, and a piece of ¼-in. or ⅜-in. ply for the bottom. Dovetail the sides and ends together, and screw the bottom on temporarily. Also make four small feet and fix these to the bottom by screwing through the ply into the feet.

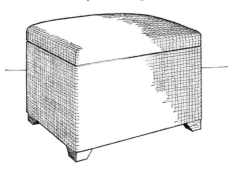

FIG. 8. USEFUL SLIPPER BOX.

The lid is a frame of 2 in. by 1 in. hardwood with a piece of 4-mm. plywood for the panel. Tenon the frame together, rebating the inside edges to take the plywood. Hinge the lid to the box. Make sure the lid fits flush all round, then remove it from the box; also the bottom.

Lining. Line the inside of the carcase with a lining or casement cloth. Begin at the bottom edge of one side, strain to the top, tacking on the edge again. Leave about ¾ in. over at each corner tacking at

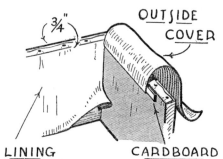

FIG. 9. LINING THE BOX.
Note how the outside cover is back-tacked.

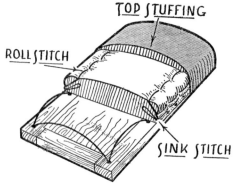

FIG. 10. UPHOLSTERING THE LID.
The roll at the edge is essential to a good shape and durable seat.

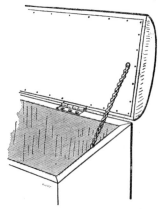

FIG. 11. HOW THE LID IS HINGED.
A chain is desirable as considerable strain is otherwise thrown on the hinges.

the top and bottom on to the edges of the ends of the carcase. Repeat this procedure at the other side, then the two ends. When finishing the ends at the corners, fold ¾ in. under and strain extra tightly to the top and bottom, creasing with the fingers whilst doing so. Cut a piece of the lining the size of the bottom and stretch this fairly tightly over the bottom opening, again tacking on the edges of the carcase. Next screw the ply bottom on over the lining.

Covering. A popular choice of covering material is leathercloth for the box and a velveteen for the seat or lid. Covering the outside is carried out in like manner. Back-tack the cover at the top on to the inside of the box about ½ in. down, as in Fig. 9. Stretch to the bottom and tack off on the underneath, neatly turning in and keeping the tacks evenly spaced. Tack the sides around the corners on to the ends before covering the ends. Treat these the same as the sides, folding inwards and creasing at the corners. If using a soft cover the corners can be stitched, but with leathercloth it is rather awkward. The side and end pieces can be cut to size and sewn, then drawn over the box. In this case the top edges cannot be back-tacked, but should be neatly gimp-pinned. Alternatively, the corners can be finished with antique nails spaced about 1 in. apart.

Treatment of lid. Tack a few loops of twine on the top about 1½ in. from the edge all round, as in Fig. 10. Pick an even amount of fibre under the loops, and fill in the centre to a thickness of approximately 2 in. Cover the stuffing with a piece of scrim, tacking it temporarily all round. Tack off finally on the top edge of the lid, making the finished height from the underside of lid to the top of the scrim about 2½ in. Stitch a roll all round, using a sink or blind stitch first and a large roll stitch next. Keep the edge of the roll level with the edge of the frame all round as shown in Fig. 10.

Second stuff with a little wool on the top of the scrim and proceed with the covering. Lay this over similarly to the scrim, temporarily tacking first. There are two methods of finishing the covering. One is to tack off the raw edge on the underside of the lid, and in this case the underside must be covered with a piece of the lining neatly fixed with gimp pins. The other method is to finish on the outside edges of the lid, doubling under when tacking off. Cover these tacks with a banding and antique nails or a gimp. With this method it is necessary to stain and polish the inside of the lid. In either case a double pleat is the best finish for the corners.

Replace the hinges and fit a short length of light chain to the inside of one end and to the underside of the lid to stay the lid when opened (see Fig. 11). Finish off by staining and polishing the feet.

A final tip, when back-tacking: place a ½-in. strip of cardboard on the cover and tack through this so that the tacks do not cut the cover when it is turned over.   Also it is much easier to keep an even line by this method (see Fig. 9).

KIDDY'S FIRESIDE CHAIR

The suggested sizes are suitable for a kiddy up to about five years of age, but can be adjusted according to size and age.   Any odd lengths of hardwood are suitable provided the two arms and the two

FIG. 12.   ATTRACTIVE CHAIR FOR THE YOUNGSTER.
Main sizes are 14½ in. wide at front, 9 in. high to seat, and 23 in. high over the back.

front legs are the same.   The front and back portions may be made up separately and joined together by the side rails and arms.   Either dowels or tenon joints may be used for the rails.   The arms are fitted to the front legs with a single large dowel, or with pins cut on the legs themselves.   Where the arms meet the back uprights, glue and screw into position.   Having completed the frame, clean up, stain and polish the arms and legs.   Frame details are given in Fig. 13.

Upholstery.   The upholstery is simple, and only small pieces of material are required.   Web the seat on the top of the seat rails,

two webs each way evenly spaced.   Strain the webs on fairly tightly
and cover them with a piece of hessian.   Use ½-in. improved tacks
for both webs and hessian, and double over all raw edges when
tacking off.   A small roll along the front edge of the seat rail will
take off the sharp edge of the wood.   Tack a 2-in. strip of hessian
along this edge on the top of the rail, allowing two-thirds of its width
to hang over the front edge.   Lay a small quantity of wool or fibre
on the hessian and turn the hessian over so as to form a roll about the
size of the little finger.   Tack this down evenly and proceed with the
stuffing of the seat.

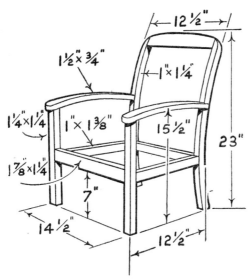

FIG. 13. DETAILS AND MAIN SIZES OF THE FRAME.

Stuffing.   Two layers of linter's felt on flock felt or better still a
piece of inch-thick foam laid on will make a nice little seat.

Covering.   For a covering material leathercloth is suitable, as it
can be sponged over, but it is rather cold when first sat upon.   Tapestry or moquette are warmer materials, but are not so easily cleaned
if anything is spilt upon them.   Measure over the seat from the outside edge of the back seat rail to under the front seat rail, pulling the
tape over tightly and adding ½ in. for turning in if using a soft
material.   (Leathercloth can be tacked off raw edge.)   Obtain the
width size by measuring from under the side rails and cut off the
material.   Make a small nick to mark the centre of both back and
front edges.

Start covering by fixing the cover with three temporary tacks on the back rail. Pull towards the front, taking care that the stuffing keeps in place. Fix at the front and also along the sides with temporary tacks. Repeat this operation once or twice until the stuffing is pulled down fairly tightly and the cover is in the correct position. Turn back each corner of the cover and carefully mark how far to cut so as to allow the cover to make a good fit round the legs. Take care with this cutting, otherwise the piece of material may be spoilt. Fold the cut edges inwards and proceed to tack off, sides first, front, and then the back edge.

Back. The back requires two pieces of web tacked on widthways and afterwards a piece of hessian similar to the seat. The webs and hessian are tacked on to the front of the back rails except at the bottom, where the hessian is left loose until the cover is tacked down. A thin, even layer of stuffing is laid upon the hessian and the cover is fixed by temporary tacking. Start at the bottom of the back by pushing the cover under the hessian and fixing it on to the top of the seat rail. Pull upwards over the stuffing and temporarily tack on the outside edge of the top back rail. Turn the cover back along the unfixed sides, and cut to fit around the arms, afterwards temporarily tacking into place.

Commence the final tacking off from the arm cuts and finishing at the bottom edge, this being tacked off from the back. The hessian which has been left loose is now tacked down in a similar manner over the cover. A good plan is to cut a thin spline of plywood or deal and nail this on to the top of the back seat rail over all the covers and hessians tacked here. This method gives a clean line to the bottom of the back.

The last item is the outside back, which can be neatly gimp-pinned along the top and two side edges of the back, and tacked on the underside of the back seat rail. Alternatively, antique or brass-headed nails, spaced about $1\frac{1}{2}$ in. apart, instead of the gimp pins will give a little decoration to the finish.

CHAPTER XI

FIRESIDE EASY CHAIR

THERE is a constant demand for items of this kind, and neither the woodwork nor the upholstery present any special difficulty.

The frame. A close-grained hardwood is needed for the frame to receive the tacks of the upholstery. Cut out the rails and uprights to shape. Assemble the back uprights and cross rails, gluing and cramping tightly; likewise the front rails and the two arm uprights. Mortise-and-tenon joints are best, but dowels are used frequently nowadays. When the glue has set add the arms and side rails. Fig. 2 gives main sizes of the frame.

FIG. I. ATTRACTIVE FIRESIDE CHAIR WHICH IS LIGHT AND TAKES UP LITTLE ROOM.

A hardwood is advisable for the frame, not only for its appearance but because it affords a good grip for the tacks and enables strong joints to be made. Front width is 20½ in. Mortise-and-tenon joints are stronger, but some prefer the simpler alternative of dowels.

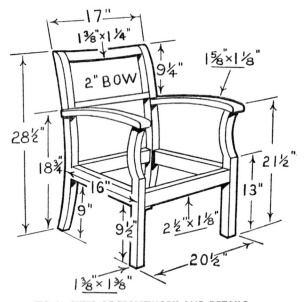

FIG. 2. SIZES OF FRAMEWORK AND DETAILS.
Hardwood should be used for all parts. Those covered with upholstery
could be of birch or beech.

**FIG. 3. POSITION OF SPRINGS ON
WEBBING OF THE CHAIR.**

A stub tenon or $\frac{3}{8}$-in. dowel can be used on the top of the arm uprights for the arm joints. At the other end of the arms a single dowel through each back upright plus a screw through the side of the arm rail into the back upright makes a sound job. Countersink for the heads of the screws, filling in afterwards with a piece of dowel. It is advisable to stain the frame and give one coat of polish before starting to upholster. Fig. 2 shows the completed framework.

Webbing. Web the seat on the underside of the seat rails, four webs from front to back and three from side to side, checked under and over. Tack on with five $\frac{5}{8}$-in. improved tacks, strain tightly with a web strainer, and tack down with four tacks. Then double over about an inch of web and tack down with two tacks.

Springs. Five 6-in. by 10-gauge springs are needed for the seat. These are positioned as shown in Fig. 3 and sewn to the webbing with three ties to each spring. The top coils of the springs are held in position with a lacing of strong laid cord. An easy and effective way is to work from corner to corner. Only two cords are required and they will cross on the centre spring. The latter should remain upright after lacing whilst the other four springs should lean a little outwards.

Cover the springs with a good-quality hessian, tacking it on with $\frac{3}{8}$-in. or $\frac{1}{2}$-in. improved tacks. Sew the tops of the springs to the hessian, using the same method as for sewing to the webs. Use three ties to each spring spaced to form a triangle.

First stuffing. A series of loops of twine are made on the hessian about 2 in. from the edges of the frame. A firm, even amount of fibre is picked under these loops. It needs to be firm and even as it will form the edge which gives shape to the seat. Fill in the centre of the seat with a thin layer of fibre or flock and cover the whole with a light hessian, or scrim. Fix this on temporarily with two or three tacks on each side.

Using a long mattress needle, form a square of ties and loops of twine. Take the ties through to the spring hessian and pull the loops tight, thereby keeping the stuffing in position. The scrim is tacked down all round keeping the stuffing even and firm, especially along the front edge.

The front edge is built up with two rows of stitching. First, a blind or sink stitch to bring the stuffing forward. Next, the top stitch, that is a through one which pulls the stuffing tightly into a small firm roll or edge about the size of a finger (see Fig. 4). The sink stitch is continued around the two sides and the back. The first stuffing completed, a top stuffing of hair or flock is required.

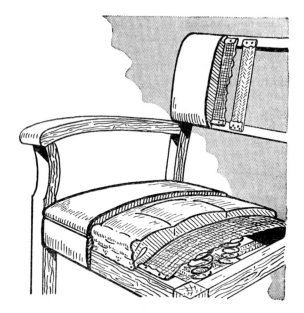

FIG. 4. SECTION THROUGH THE UPHOLSTERY.

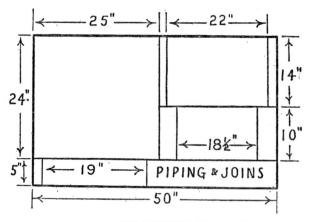

FIG. 5. CUTTING PLAN USING 50-in. MATERIAL.

Second stuffing. This is picked under several loops of twine made across the seat. The idea is to form an even, rounded mould of stuffing about 1½ in. in thickness.

Cover. Cutting the cover is the next item, the sizes given in the plan in Fig. 5 being approximate and useful as a guide. It is advisable, however, to measure and check on the actual chair. If hair is used for the top stuffing a piece of wadding should be laid over it before the cover is pulled on. Fix the cover on the back rail with three temporary tacks and strain over the stuffing to the underside of the roll or edge, fixing there with three or four skewers. Likewise fix along each side rail with temporary tacks.

When it is nicely in position turn back the corners and carefully cut for the uprights. Turn in at these cuts and pull down, tacking off neatly on the underneath of the side and back rails. Under the front edge the cover is finished by stitching to the scrim with a fine twine used in a half-circular needle.

A piece of piping is sewn along the top edge of the border, which is then stitched in place slightly above the line of stitches holding the seat cover. Place a little flock or linter's felt under the border and finish by tacking off on the underside of the seat rail. One or two gimp pins can be used to hold the cover at the points adjoining the polished parts of the frame.

The back. One piece of webbing strained tightly from the bottom back rail to the top is required. Next, a piece of hessian is tacked and strained on as tightly as possible. A single thin layer of stuffing is picked on the hessian and the cover pulled over it. Temporarily tack first, working into position before finally tacking off on the backs of the rails forming the back. This completed, the outside back can be tacked on with gimp pins or fixed with temporary tacks, then slip-stitched in position. A light hessian bottom tacked on to cover the web completes the upholstery.

FINE QUALITY REPRODUCTION CHAIR AND SETTEE OF THE FIRST HALF 18th CENTURY.

CHAPTER XII

CUSHION SEAT EASY CHAIR

A POPULAR type is the medium-sized, deep-sprung easy chair. That shown in Fig. 1 is of modern design, upholstered by the hand-sprung method, though patent springing could be used if preferred. Birch is the recognized wood for upholstery frames, but any fairly close-grained hardwood will serve.

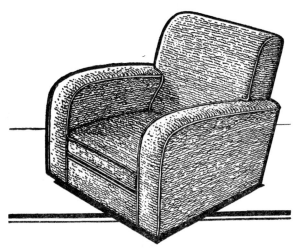

FIG. I. A MOST COMFORTABLE FORM OF EASY CHAIR.
This is fitted with a loose cushion made specially for the chair and either feather filled or of the pocketed spring type.

Frame joints. Use $\frac{3}{8}$-in. birch or beech dowels on all joints, three dowels on the main rails, two elsewhere, excepting the side tacking rails which only require one each. The back framing can be assembled, glued, and cramped up tightly. Likewise the two front arm uprights and the front seat rails. Join these two sections together with the side seat rails and top arm rails.

The small tacking rails at the sides are dowelled to the arm uprights with a single dowel and housed into the back uprights. Fit the two back tacking rails as tightly as possible before dowelling with two dowels at each end. If these rails are housed into the side tacking rails about ⅛ in. it will prevent their turning when the web-bing, etc. is strained. Glue and screw brackets to each of the bottom corners; these will brace the frame and enable a ⅜-in. hole to be bored to take the castors. Fig. 2 shows the completed framework.

Webbing and springing. Turn the frame upside down, resting the front rail on a trestle or other firm support. Start the webbing from the centre of the front rail, using six webs from front to back. The five side-to-side webs are interlaced under and over the front-to-back webbing. When tacking on the web turn over about 1 in.

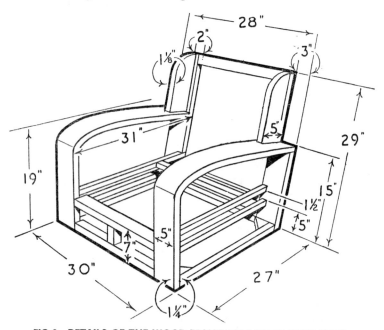

FIG. 2. DETAILS OF THE WOOD FRAMEWORK WITH MAIN SIZES.

and use five ⅝-in. improved tacks. Stretch tightly with a web strainer to the back rail and tack down with four tacks first, then turn over about 1 in. and tack down with two tacks.

When the seat webbing is completed place the frame on trestles or a bench. Turn the frame on one side and tack two pieces of web to the arm tacking rail. Space them an equal distance apart and strain to the top arm rail. A piece of hessian is next tacked on, working from the bottom rail to the top rail and from the back upright to the front arm upright. Double over the bottom edge and tack on, then strain to the top, tacking through the single thickness first.

[Photograph by courtesy Contemporary Furniture (Enfield) Ltd.

THE LURASHELL "ANGELINA" MK. II THREE-SEATER SETTEE AND ARMCHAIR WITH GLASS FIBRE MOULDS.

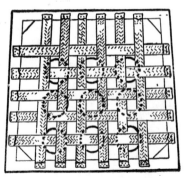

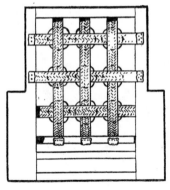

FIG. 3. LAY-OUT OF WEBBING AND SPRINGS FOR THE SEAT.   **FIG. 4. BACK WEBBING AND SPRINGS (BACK VIEW).**

Note how the up-and-down webs are tacked on to the back of the tacking rail and brought round to the front before straining to the top rail. Also that the bottom side-to-side web is tacked to the front of the back uprights.

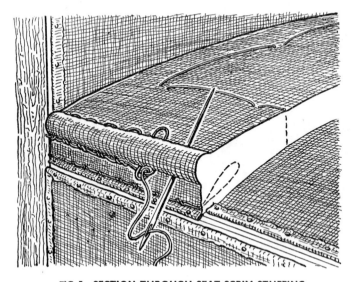

FIG. 5. SECTION THROUGH SEAT SCRIM STUFFING.

Note the running through stitches and method of stitching roll or edge.

This is afterwards turned over and tacked.   Complete both arms and set the frame upright ready for sewing the springs to the seat webbing.   Nine 9-in. by 9-gauge springs spaced as shown in Fig. 3 will form a good seat.   They are sewn in with a spring needle and twine, starting with a slip-knot and continuing with three ties to each spring, the ties forming a rough triangle.   Continue the twine from spring to spring, keeping it taut from tie to tie.   This completed, the tops of the spring are "laced" or lashed in position with a laid cord or stout sisal twine.

Lacing the Springs.   Knock a ⅜-in. improved tack partly home opposite each row of springs on the seat-tacking rails and the front rail.   Tie a piece of laid cord round each tack on the back rail and on one side rail, and drive the tacks home.   Start with the centre row of springs and bring the laid cord from the back rail to the second top coil of the nearest spring.   Make a hitch round the coil and continue to the other side of the spring, making another hitch, this time on the top coil.   Continue to the centre and front springs, coming down to the front rail.

Follow this method with each row, back to front, and side to side, keeping the centre spring upright and all the others pitched slightly outwards.   Cover the springs with a good-quality hessian tacked to the seat-tacking rails with ⅜-in. or ½-in. improved tacks.   The tops of the springs are also sewn to the spring hessian with three ties.

The first or scrim stuffing.   Make two loops of twine across the front edge.   The edge stuffing is picked under these twines, but first cut a piece of scrim for the seat and tuck one edge down the back of the seat.   Fix it on the edge of the tacking rail with three or four tacks and throw the rest over the back, clear of the seat.   Push sufficient fibre to form a fairly firm stuffing between the tacking rails and under the front loops.   Pick a thin layer of stuffing over the springs in the centre of the seat, merging it with the fibre already in place.   Pull the scrim over, fixing it on all rails with temporary tacks. Make a square of running-through stitches, one short and one long, to hold the stuffing in place.   The front edge is finished off next; this may require the addition of a little more fibre, as it is tacked off, to make a firm, even edge.

A sink, or blind, stitch and a top stitch will be sufficient to build up an edge to the required height.   Make the blind stitch almost on the scrim tacking-off tacks.   Starting with a slip-knot on the left side of the front, continue by inserting the needle about 2 in. ahead of the knot.   Do not take the needle quite through the scrim, but return it midway between the starting knot and the point of insertion. Make a double twist round the needle with the twine as it is removed and pull taut. Continue in this manner across the front edge, first with the blind stitch, then with a top stitch. This is made in the same way, except that the needle is pulled right through before returning. Complete the tacking off of the scrim, thus finishing the first stuffing of the seat (Fig. 5).

Back. The back is the next item. This is webbed with three webs from side to side and three from bottom to top. Six 6-in. by 12-gauge springs are required for the two top rows, and three 6-in.

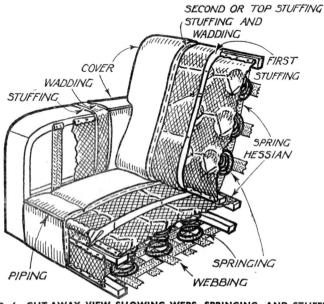

FIG. 6. CUT-AWAY VIEW SHOWING WEBS, SPRINGING, AND STUFFINGS.

by 10-gauge for the bottom row of springs (see Fig. 4). These are sewn to the webbing in the usual manner, but are not laced on the tops. Only the top row of springs is pulled slightly upwards by a piece of laid cord passed through and round the middle coil of each spring. The ends of the cord are fixed to the top rail with ⅝-in. improved tacks.

Measure over the springs for the hessian size and fix this with temporary tacks all round.

Place the springs in position by moving them from the rear through the webbing. They should all slant a little towards the top of the chair and the outer ones towards the sides of the frame. Hold them in place for sewing by inserting skewers through the hessian under the top coils. Sew to the hessian with a good twine, using the method already described. Make several loops of twine across the top and down the sides to the top of the arms. Pick an even amount of fibre under these loops, also across the bottom portion of the back. Fill in the centre part with a thin layer of fibre. Cover with scrim and "run through" with twine in a similar fashion to that used in doing the seat. Tack down on the back tacking rail, and along each side rail. The top edges above the arms are tacked and stitched with a sink and a top stitch to form a roll about the size of one's finger. Finally tack the scrim off evenly along the top rail. The sectional view in Fig. 6 gives a good idea of how the upholstery is built up.

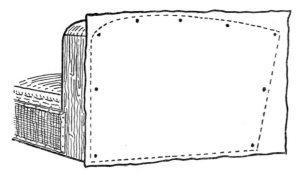

FIG. 7. OUTSIDE ARM FIXED TEMPORARILY FOR MARKING OUT AND CUTTING.

Cutting the cover. The covering for this chair requires careful planning before cutting, especially if it is a patterned material. Select the most prominent part of the pattern and make it a centre *motif* for both the cushion and the inside back. Approximately 4½ yards of 50-in. material are required. Measure each section of the chair with a tape-measure. Fig. 10 shows a cutting plan for the cover. The sizes are approximate and will serve as a guide. It is advisable to measure all sections of the chair before cutting. Also, if using a patterned material the sequence of cutting may have to be varied. For example, it might be advisable to cut the inside arms first, followed by a cushion border, thereby getting a central design for the inside back without wasting material. It is by careful measurement and the planning of each "cut" beforehand that wastage is avoided, an important matter in these expensive days. Note that the *Back* shown at the right at the top is the O back.

The seat, inside arms, and inside back are flyed, that is, odd pieces of cheap material are sewn to the main covers where they merge between the seat and back and all unseen parts. It is customary to use a piece of lining or other inexpensive but strong material on the platform of the seat under the cushion. Draw a parallel line with pencil or chalk 5 in. from the front edge of the seat. The seat platform is sewn to the scrim along this line. The front part of the seat will require a piece of cover approximately 6½ in. by the half width and this is sewn to the platform lining.

If necessary the lining can be flyed, but generally it is not worth the trouble unless material is short. Insert a piece of piping between the front border and the seat when joining together. Shape the seat piece slightly before sewing, as the stuffing is always a little less at the ends near the arms.

Place one of the outside arm pieces in position on the chair as in Fig. 7, tacking it there temporarily and marking round it with a piece of chalk. Cut to this shape, allowing $\frac{3}{8}$–$\frac{1}{2}$ in. all round for sewing. This arm can now be used as a template to cut the other outside arm and both inside arms. The inside back is also fixed in place temporarily with tacks and skewers. Mark round the back facings and where the back meets the inside arms. The back facings are also offered up and skewered in place. These can be cut to shape on the job. Make several notches on both the facings and the back where they meet. These will be a guide when the back is ready for sewing.

Remove the back and facings, trimming them evenly round the edges, but do not cut out the notches. Finish cutting where the arms meet the back, making a small allowance for the stuffing of each arm. The arm stuffing will be quite light, so do not cut away too much. A narrow strip is cut for each of these sides to form a collar (see Fig. 8) and the back is ready for sewing.

All the sewing work can be assembled and some piping cut and made up ready for inserting as the sewing proceeds. The arms are piped along both sides of the top arm pieces as the inside and outside arms are joined to them. The inside back is piped round the back facings and the arm cut-outs. Another piece of piping is across the front of the seat. Two small joins will be needed on the lower part of the outside back.

Covering. Stretch the seam of the lining and seat front piece along the pencil line on the scrim and fix in place with several skewers. Sew this seam to the scrim with a circular needle and twine, making running stitches about 1 in. in length. A single run of twine is made across the front part, and two across the back part of the seat, making two or three loops in each. A light layer of stuffing, hair if possible, is worked under these twines and evenly "picked out." A piece of wadding is required over all hair stuffing before covering, and this applies throughout the job. The covering over the platform is tucked down between the arms and back openings and tacked off on the tacking rails. Strain this cover sufficiently to remove all wrinkles and creases before tacking off. The front of the seat and border are dealt with next. It is advisable to strain these on as tight as possible to obtain a neat finish.

Arms. The arms are next in order, but before commencing to cover, tack a piece of light hessian over the outside to form a lining

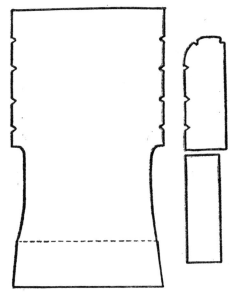

FIG. 8. DIAGRAM OF INSIDE BACK, BACK FACING, AND COLLAR PIECE. ALSO METHOD OF NOTCHING FOR GUIDANCE WHEN JOINING TOGETHER.

or backing to the outside arm covering. Stretch, and tack it on as tightly as possible from the front to the back and along the top arm rail, but leave the bottom loose; also a few inches up on each side so that the tacking rails are accessible.

A series of twine loops along the top arms and the same from back to front across the inside arms is needed for a light layer of stuffing in each place. This stuffing is covered with wadding which can be continued over the outside arm lining to give a better finish if so desired. The cover is carefully laid over the stuffing and gradually moved into position so that temporary tacks can fix the piping cords at each end. Once this has been done the flys can be tucked away and temporarily tacked. Smooth out all round and work into place, finishing off by putting a good strain on the piped seams. Tack down the inside arms, the outside arm linings, and finally the outside arm coverings.

Back. The inside back "fly" is tucked away through the seat opening, and the remainder of the back laid over the seat whilst the stuffing proceeds. About four twines across the back are required as stuffing twines. Pick an even layer of stuffing under them, a little thicker at the bottom to give a slight swelling to support the small of

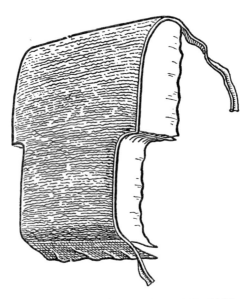

FIG. 9. INSIDE BACK ASSEMBLED AND SEWN
READY FOR FIXING IN PLACE.

the back when sitting in the chair. Cover with wadding, and bring the covering up and over the top of the back. Smooth the work out gradually until the piping round the arms and the facings falls into place. The facings are padded out with a little wool or odd pieces of wadding pushed in from the back edge before tacking off. When tacking down strain to clear all puckers, etc., but not so tight as to spoil the shape of the back. Tack round the facings first, then the fly and lastly the top edge.

The outside back will complete the covering. If the cover is a thin material, a hessian lining is advisable. In any case it gives a better finish. Fix the outside back all round with temporary tacks, pulling taut and doubling under the edges. Afterwards finish by slip-stitching with a half-circular needle and strong thread. A hessian bottom is tacked over the webs, the edges being doubled under and finished about ½ in. from the edges of the frame.

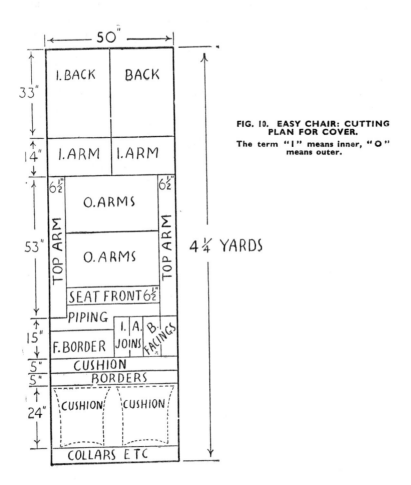

FIG. 10. EASY CHAIR: CUTTING PLAN FOR COVER.

The term "I" means inner, "O" means outer.

Cushion. The cushion for a chair of this type can be of latex foam, polyether foam, or be a spring interior cushion. Foam 3 in. to 3½ in. thick of either variety will form quite a good seating unit giving a neat, clean finished cushion. Feather-filled cushions are also comfortable although not so clean lined as the newer foams.

7—P.U.

Cutting the cushion case. It is necessary to take a template of the seat. A piece of stiff paper will suffice. After cutting this lay it on the cover and mark round it, allowing about $\frac{3}{8}$ or $\frac{1}{2}$ in. for sewing on each side. The width of material can be folded and the two pieces for the top and the bottom cut together. Four borders are also required. A cutting width of $4\frac{1}{2}$ in. makes a nice depth of cushion for feathers. If it is intended to use a spring interior eventually it is advisable to cut the borders 5 in. wide. Feathers require an inside case of waxed or down-proofed calico. This is cut a full inch larger all round than the outside case.

Cut the borders to fit the case so that the joins are at each corner and sew all the pieces together with piping inserted. Leave a hand-hole at the back for filling purposes, sewing this up when filled. The inside case is cut and sewn in a similar manner and then filled. Close and sew the hand-hole and insert the inner case into the outer, pushing the corners well into the corners of the outer case. Neatly sew up the "hand-hole" and the cushion can be placed in the chair, thus completing the job.

CHAPTER XIII

HAMMOCK CHAIR

THE term "hammock" is often used to describe chairs with the seat and back made in a continuous curve. They are generally of the larger fireside type and are comfortable in use. The sizes given in Fig. 2 may be varied slightly, but do not make the width between the arms less than 1 ft. 6 in. Make up the seat and back

FIG. I. THE HAMMOCK CHAIR IN WHICH SEAT AND BACK ARE CONTINUOUS.
This type of chair comes midway between the fireside and the easy chair. It is larger than the former but smaller than the fully upholstered easy.

parts first, using birch for preference. The arms are fitted next, and these may be screwed from the inside of the rails. Another method is to fix with $\frac{1}{4}$-in. bolts through, the heads being sunk and filled in later. Stain and partly polish the arms before commencing to upholster.

93

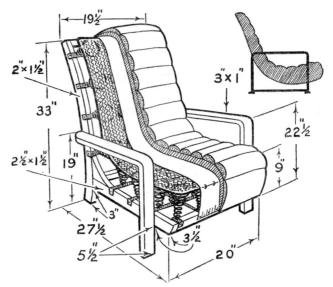

FIG. 2. CUT-AWAY VIEW SHOWING SPRINGING.
A specially made spring unit is used.

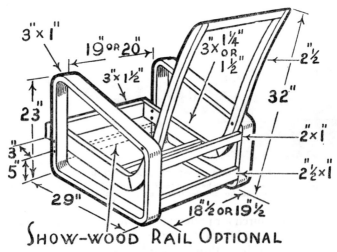

FIG. 3. CONSTRUCTION OF A MODERN FORM OF CHAIR.
This is an alternative design of frame in which arms are of bentwood
made as a continuous loop.

Fig. 3 gives an alternative form of framework. All the frame joints should be dowelled; three ⅜-in. dowels well glued and cramped up tightly make a very strong joint. The arms are generally attached to the frame by bolts through both arms and framing. Alternatively the frame rails can be let into the arms about ¼ in., then glued and screwed from the inside of the frame rails. The two back rails joining the arms together should be polished. Additional strength is gained by adding a further polished rail across the front below the seat framing.

Springing. Several forms of springing can be used, the type illustrated in Fig. 2 being suitable. These units are usually made to customer's own requirements, so that it is necessary to give details when ordering. Size and style of frame, height and gauge of springs are the main items. The back springs should be lighter than the seat springing. A suitable seat size is 6-in. by 10-gauge, and for the back 5-in. by 12-gauge.

The metal laths are fixed to the frame with clout nails or small wall nails. If the laths are a trifle long bend them round the frame and hammer down. Before covering the springs with hessian it is advisable to consider the method of stuffing.

Stuffing. Hair and fibre can be obtained needled on to hessian, but some of the hessian used is very light in weave. When this is the case it is best to cover the springs first with a fair quality hessian. This also is necessary if Hairlok, loose fibre, or hair is used.

Tack the hessian on with ½-in. improved tacks, keeping the threads square and doubling under the raw edge. The wire forming the frame around the top of the unit is caught to the hessian with a series of stitches. Start with a slip-knot, then take the twine along about 3 in. and make a half-hitch round the wire and through the hessian. Proceed all round the unit in this manner. The hair or fibre pad is laid over the hessian and tacked down on the outside edge of the frame. These pads of stuffing are the easiest method to use with this class of chair. Generally a little extra hair or fibre is desirable on the seat.

Covering. The fluted style of covering is popular in hammock chairs, although some are finished plain with three buttons where the seat and back meet. Measure across the width of the seat from one edge of the spring unit to the other plus ½ in. each side for sewing. Next measure the length from the outside edge of the top back rail to 1½ in. under the front seat rail. The fluted divisions can be made any reasonable size, about 4 in. being usual. Add 1 in. for each division to the measured seat and back length, then chalk out the sizes on this piece of cover. Obtain a piece of calico and mark out similarly, only each space to be a ½ in. narrower.

Machine the cover to the calico at each marking, thus forming a pocket at each division. Insert into these pockets a layer of linter's felt. There are several methods used to do this. The felt can be wrapped round a piece of ply and pushed through, or two pieces of thin ply used to compress the felt and push it through. A piece of web can be tacked to a strip of ply at one end and the linter's felt laid on the ply. The web is pulled over the felt and held tight whilst the ply is pushed through the pocket. Draw the web out at the other

FIG. 4. CENTRE COVER AND BORDER NOTCHED FOR JOINING TOGETHER.

FIG. 5. HOW POCKETS ARE FORMED.

end then withdraw the ply, leaving the felt in place. This latter method is quite useful if a small quantity of hair is first placed on the ply under the felt.

Temporarily secure this portion of the cover on to the chair with skewers. Also cut and fit the side borders, marking both borders and centre cover with small notches at short intervals (Fig. 4). Remove the pieces from the job and stitch together with a piping between the notches giving the correct positions. After completing this lay the cover over the chair and, starting where the seat and back meet, temporarily fix all round. Work away from this centre and after fixing commence tacking off in the same way. This final tacking is all done on the back edges of the frame rails with $\frac{3}{8}$-in. or $\frac{1}{2}$-in. fine tacks. Fix the outside back covering with temporary tacks, afterwards sewing it with a half-circular needle and thread; alternatively gimp pins can be used. The seat is finished off with a hessian or black linen bottom neatly and evenly tacked.

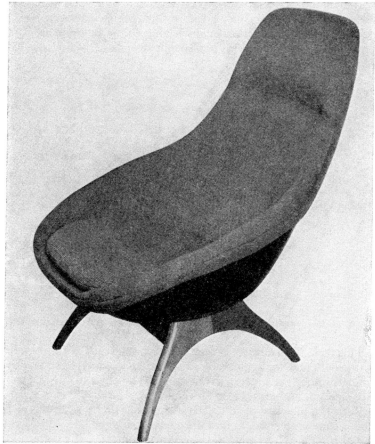

[Photograph by courtesy Contemporary Furniture (Enfield) Ltd.

LURASHELL BEVERLEY PLUS CHAIR WITH FIBRE GLASS SHELL

CHAPTER XIV

FIRESIDE CHAIR

DURING recent years new ideas and inventions have been tried out in the majority of crafts. In the upholstery trade most of these efforts have been made with a view to improving the springing of chairs and settees. Some of the ideas have been successful, others not so good. Among the former, cable or tension springs used in conjunction with cushions having spring interiors are a real contribution to comfortable upholstery, particularly the fireside chair.

FIG. I. THE FRAME CONSTRUCTION AND METHOD OF UPHOLSTERING THIS CHAIR ARE EXPLAINED BELOW.

This style of small easy is very popular, especially with the ladies, as it is light and easily moveable, also taking up much less room than its big brother the modern divan easy. The chair in Fig. 1 gives a nice size seat and makes a comfortable job.

With the majority of upholstered frames, birch or beech are the woods commonly used, as they are cheap, make good dowelled joints, and also stain well to most of the popular colours. If a better job is required use birch for the covered parts of the chair, and oak, mahogany, or walnut for the arms and front legs. The sizes in Fig. 2 may be varied a little, but bear in mind the general proportions.

Framework. Dowelling is the usual trade method with most joints on upholstered chair frames and is quite effective when carefully done, but, of course, a mortise-and-tenon joint can be used if preferred. Make a template of ply or cardboard for the back uprights and draw out a full-size plan of the seat. Mark out carefully the seat

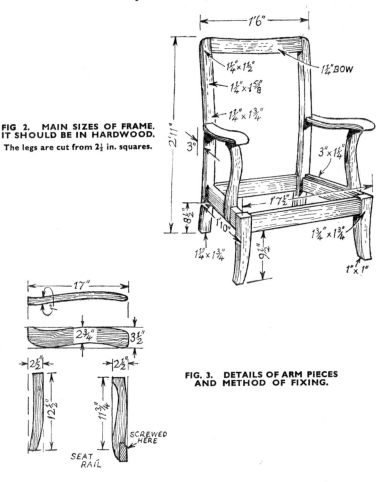

FIG 2. MAIN SIZES OF FRAME.
IT SHOULD BE IN HARDWOOD.
The legs are cut from 2½ in. squares.

FIG. 3. DETAILS OF ARM PIECES
AND METHOD OF FIXING.

rails, noting the angles of the side rails. Cut off all these rails, also the curved top back rail, and prepare for jointing. Also rebate the side seat rails ⅜ in. deep and ½ in. wide on the inside to take the spring fixings.

Assemble the back framework first. Glue and cramp up firmly.

Follow with the front seat rail and the front legs and allow the glue to set before joining the back framing to the front. Two cramps are an advantage when putting the side rails in.

Now cut two further templates for the arm pieces, shaping them as in Fig. 3. Prepare and cut the arms, fitting them carefully before finally fixing. It is a good method to glue and screw these to the seat rail and back upright respectively, jointing up first with two dowels at the top joint where the arm meets its upright or stump. Screw from the inside of the frame, notching out a little of the arm stump to enable it to fit the seat rail squarely (Fig. 3).

Leave the frame until the glue is properly set and then clean up the arms and legs with glass-paper before staining to the desired shade. You may now polish up to the final rubber if you wish, or leave the polishing until the upholstering is finished. In any case it is advisable to leave the finishing rubber until everything is done so that any scratches can be dealt with.

Springing the back. Having completed the frame the upholstering of it is the next job. It will be best to start with the back. This can be sprung with cable springs if desired, but it is not absolutely necessary. If it is not being sprung, strain two webs from bottom to top and one web, not too tightly strained, across the centre from side to side. Then hessian in the ordinary way, tacking it on and turning over the raw edges.

It would hardly be practicable to spring a small back like the one being described with the vertical coil spring, so this is an occasion when the cable or tension spring is useful. These springs are horizontal in action. They are stretched from side to side on the frame and expand when in use, whereas the coil spring compresses. The term cable spring is probably given to them because of their likeness to a piece of cable, whereas tension springing accurately describes the method.

Fix them to the back as shown in Fig. 4, using either a clout nail or a staple to attach the link to the frame. The spring and the two links are usually obtainable in a 16½-in. standard size, and should be fixed with an initial stretch of about 1½ in., so for the back you will probably have to cut a little off the spring or do away with the links at each end. Starting about 2 in. from the top rail, space the springs evenly apart, the last one about 6 in. from the bottom rail. Seven springs are sufficient.

Next proceed to hessian the back; it must not be tightly stretched on but allowed to sag so that sufficient play is allowed for the movement of the springs. Tack the hessian with ⅜-in. improved tacks, doubling over the edges.

Back stuffing. There are several ways of stuffing the back: Rubberized hair or fibre makes a good job with tension springing. This is cut to the size and laid on the hessian, then covered with wadding. Another method is to tack a little roll round the top and two sides, filling in the centre with hair or fibre. To form the roll, tack a piece of hessian about 2½ in. wide on to the front of the side and top rails, allowing 2 in. of the hessian to hang outside the rails (see Fig. 5). When this is done start at the centre of the top and lay enough fibre to make a firm roll as thick as a finger upon the hessian, turn the latter over the fibre and tack down as shown in Fig. 5. Proceed all round, keeping the hessian tight from tack to tack and the stuffing an even thickness. This is an awkward little job, but with practice it will become quite easy.

FIG. 4. FIXING CABLE SPRINGS.

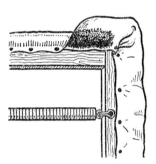

FIG. 5. METHOD OF MAKING THE ROLL OR EDGE.

When this has been completed place loops of twine round the edges approximately 2 in. inwards, and further loops about 6 in. from the first ones along each side. Pick some hair or fibre evenly under these loops, making a 2-in. thickness of stuffing all over the back. Cut a piece of calico the over-all size of the back and lay this over the stuffing. Fix with three temporary tacks at the bottom of the back and stretch to the top, fixing there with three half-driven tacks.

Now turn the calico back along the unfixed sides and cut to fit round the arms; then turn down and temporarily tack at each side. The calico can now be tacked off, starting at the bottom and proceeding in the same order as when temporarily tacking. Turn in at the bottom, but tack the raw edge round the other sides. Note that all the tacking off of the hessian, calico, and final cover must be done within about 1 in. from the top edge of the bottom seat rail, as this makes for a neat finish.

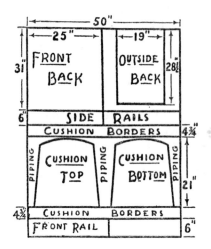

FIG. 6. LAY-OUT COVER WITH
APPROXIMATE SIZES.

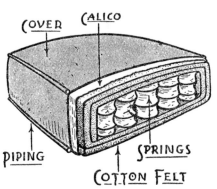

FIG. 7. SECTION THROUGH
CUSHION SHOWING SPRING
INTERIOR.

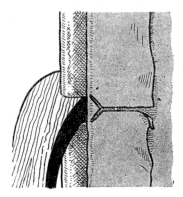

FIG. 8. METHOD OF CUTTING
AROUND THE ARM.

The cushion. Leave the chair now and proceed with the cushion. This you can obtain ready made in calico, but if you prefer to make it yourself obtain a spring unit either of the calico-pocketed type or a hessian-covered one. The springs of either kind measure approximately 3 in. across the top, so you will require one containing six springs one way and five the other. Make a rough paper template of the seat—that is, where the cushion is to fit—and allow about 1 in. extra all round.

You can make the cushion up straightway in its final cover, but a calico case first will be found easier, especially for the homeworker. Place the template on the calico and cut two pieces to its size; also four borders 5 in. wide to go round the sides. Machine the borders all round one piece, then machine the other to the front border only.

A thick felt made of waste cotton linters is the usual stuffing. Cover the spring unit all over with two thicknesses of this felt and place the whole in the calico case. This will appear an unwieldy mass, but by compressing it with one hand and pulling the top calico over with the other until it meets the border, then holding it there with a few skewers, you will be able to slip-stitch the top to the border, thus completing the cushion (see Fig. 11). Instead of a spring interior, foamed latex or polyether foam units can be used. Cut the borders according to the thickness of the cushion unit.

Cushion cover. Two and one-eighth yards of 50-in. material are required. Before cutting into the cover take your rough cushion template and cut it accurately to the size of the seat, allowing only ½ in. all round. Measure the templates, allow two 4¾ in. off the full width of the cover for the borders; measure the inside and outside back and allow two widths 6 in. wide for covering the seat rails. Lining or black linen will also be required to lie over the seat springs.

Cut the front and outside backs off together, also the top and bottom of the cushion, cutting the latter two by the template. The cushion will have to be machined all round the top and bottom excepting for an opening at the back for putting the calicoed unit in. Make up a piping of the waste pieces of cover by cutting them into 1¼-in. wide strips joined together, and machine up with a piece of piping cord in them. When making the cushion case insert this piping between the seams at the top and bottom and you will have a first-class finish (Fig. 7).

Chair covering. To return to the covering of the chair itself, mark the centre of your inside back cover with a small nick top and bottom and fix at the bottom and the top similarly to the calico, first laying a piece of wadding over the calico. Mark carefully and cut round the arms, making quite sure of these cuts as they are not

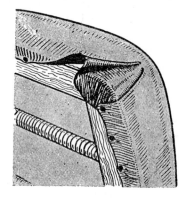

FIG. 9. MAKING TOP CORNER PLEATS ON THE BACK.

FIG. 10. HOW FRONT CORNERS ARE FINISHED.

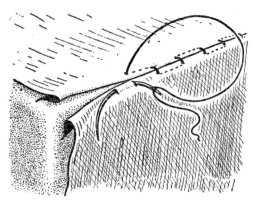

FIG. 11. MAKING SLIP-STITCH.

too easy (Fig. 8). Fix with temporary tacks down each side and then commence tacking off, top, bottom, sides, and the top corners last of all. The top corners should come out very clean if finished with a double pleat (Fig. 9).

Seat springing. The fixing of the seat springs has been left to this stage so that they have not been in the way when tacking off at the bottom of the back. Start fixing them 2 in. from the front rail and 2 in. apart, nine in all. With the piece of lining or black linen already mentioned make a $\frac{1}{2}$-in. hem on two sides and a 2-in. slot on the other two, placing the first and last springs into these slots, the lining coming over the top of the other springs, thus making a neat finish.

When all the springs are in place and securely fixed, start covering the seat rails, the side ones first. Stretch the cover from front to back along the top of the side rails, placing a temporary tack at each end and allowing enough to go round the back and front legs. Turn under and tack down on the rebated part of the rail with $\frac{3}{8}$-in. or $\frac{1}{2}$-in. gimp pins. Cut round the arms carefully and, placing the chair on its side, stretch the cover over the rail, fixing it with three or four tacks on the underside. Finally tack off with gimp pins, turning the raw edge under. Make a cut at both leg joints and bring the cover round the legs, tacking off on the front and back legs respectively.

The remaining front rail must now be covered; this time tack on the inside of the rail about $\frac{1}{2}$ in. down, either with gimp pins or by back-tacking. That is, lay the cover on with the wrong side upwards and then cut a strip of cardboard $\frac{1}{2}$ in. wide and tack through that and the cover. Turn the cover back and over the rail, tacking off at the bottom the same as on the side rails. Fold the ends of this piece in so that they form a pleat at the centre of the front legs (see Fig. 10), fixing at the bottom with one gimp pin and slip-stitching together later.

Outside back cover. The last piece of cover is the outside back. Fix this on all round with temporary tacks, turning in the raw edge of the material, and slip-stitch this around the top and two sides with thread and a half-circular needle. Whilst the needle and thread are in action finish off the front corners, also the cushion opening, then tack off the outside back at the bottom rail. Turn the chair upside down, knock four domes of silence on the legs, and give the polished portions a final rubber.

CHAPTER XV

WING ARMCHAIR

BIRCH or beech is the most suitable wood for the frame, with walnut or mahogany for the front legs. Sizes and the general details are given in Fig. 2. A larger chair can be built up from these details, but the height of the seat and the arms from the floor should remain the same. The main seat joints require three or four $\frac{5}{16}$-in. or $\frac{3}{8}$-in. dowels each, whilst two will be sufficient at the other joints.

FIG. 1. WING ARMCHAIR IN WALNUT STYLE.
Although the main outline of the chair is on period
lines, the upholstery is in the modern manner.

Braces glued and screwed into the seat corners will add to the rigidity of the frame. Before fitting the side seat rails rebate the inside top edges $\frac{3}{8}$ in. deep and $\frac{1}{2}$ in. wide for receiving the springs. After assembling the frame stain the legs and top, bottom, and inside edges of the seat rails.

Webbing. Start by webbing the arms, one web across the centre of each arm and another about 1 in. away from the back upright. Stretch on tightly and keep the end webs parallel with the uprights.

Next tack a piece of hessian to the bottom tacking rail, strain to the top arm rail and tack off. At the end near the back upright fold the hessian over and sew it to the web with twine. Tack off the remaining end of the hessian on to the front upright.

The back can be either of the firm type or sprung with tension springs. If the former, stretch two webs from the bottom to the top and two crossways, spaced at equal distances and tacked on the front edges of the rails. The hessian is tacked on also from bottom to top, then along the sides, but do not strain too tightly sideways. If a spring back is desired fit seven cable springs equal distances apart, starting about 6 in. from the seat rail. Fix these to the back

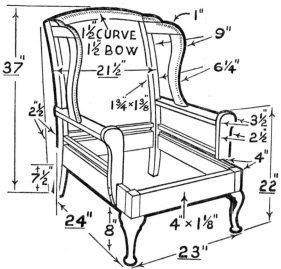

FIG. 2. SIZES AND DETAILS OF FRAME.

uprights with staples or clout nails. Cover with hessian tacked on as for a firm back but with a certain amount of sag to allow for the movement of the springs.

Coming to the actual stuffing of the back there are several alternatives. Hairlok and fibre or hair woven on to hessian can be obtained cut to size and are simply tacked down at a few points to hold them in place. Otherwise a few loops of twine can be run across the hessian and loose fibre or hair picked under them. Start at the bottom with a thickness of about 3 in. graduating to nothing at the top. Cover with scrim and run through with a needle and twine, making long stitches and forming an oblong in the centre of the back. The space

8—P.U.

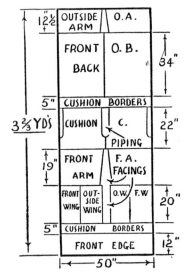

**FIG. 3.   APPROXIMATE COVER
LAY-OUT.**

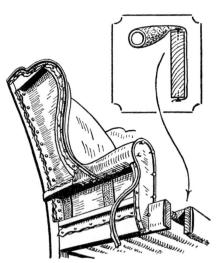

**FIG. 4.   TACKING OFF AND FINISHING
DETAILS.**

Inset is shown a section through front seat
rail and first cable spring.

on the top of the arm rail also requires filling in with a little stuffing and covering with scrim.

Cutting the cover. For the cover 3⅝ yards of 50-in. material are required, this allowing for a reversible cushion. Take a rough template of the cushion size and carefully measure the other parts of the chair before cutting. The approximate sizes and a suggested scheme of cutting are shown in Fig. 3. This may have to be re-arranged according to the pattern and material chosen. If the design has a prominent feature it should be centred on both the inside back and the seat cushion.

Cover the arms first. These require little stuffing; just a layer of linter's felt will be sufficient. Tuck the cover through the opening between the arm tacking rail and the seat, and fix with temporary tacks. Pull the cover over the arm and fix it on to the underside of the arm rail. Smooth out sideways and temporarily fix at the back and the front uprights. Make sure the cover is in the correct position then cut round the wing upright.

Finish off each arm and proceed with the back in a similar manner. If this has been first stuffed as described, a thin top stuffing of hair or wool is necessary. The cover is tacked off on the front of the uprights and on the back of the curved top rail.

Covering the wings. The wings are a little more awkward as the bottom edges of the cover are tacked on to the top of the arm rails, and the position must be carefully judged. The cover is tacked through the wrong side similarly to back-tacking, then laid over the arms whilst the wings are hessianed. Tack the hessian over the top of the cover on to the arms and on to the front of the wings. Do not fix to the back uprights until the covering is finished. A thin layer of hair covered with a thickness of linter's felt will be about the right quantity of stuffing. Bring the cover over this stuffing and fix on the outside edges of the wings. With a little careful manipulating the fulness can be worked out quite clean round the curved edges. When this has been done finally tack off. Also tack the back edges on to the inside of the back uprights and finish the hessian here too.

Seat springing. The seat tension springs can now be fixed in position, eight in all, spaced about 2 in. apart. Cover the two small side pieces of seat rail before covering the front rail. Back-tack this latter piece of cover along the top edge of the front rail. Pass the loose edge under the first spring and bring it up between the first and second springs. Lay a piece of linter's felt along the space between the first spring and the edge, afterwards pulling the cover over the front and tacking off on the underside of the front rail. This is shown inset in Fig. 4.

Make up some piping and tack pieces round the front facings, along the outside edges of the wings and across the top of the outside back. The outside wings, arms, back, and front facings are now tacked on in the order given. Temporarily tack where they make contact with the piping, afterwards sewing with thread and a half-circular needle.

Cushion. The cushion can be either a spring interior or foam-filled unit. If making a single cushion at home it would be advisable to make up the spring interior type in a calico case. Cut the calico case and stitch up, then wrap two thicknesses of linter's felt round the unit and place it in the case. Fill up the front corners with odd pieces of stuffing and sew up the case. Correct the seat template and cut the cushion cover by it, also cut pieces for the cushion borders. The cushion cover is machined together and the case containing the springs, etc., inserted through an opening left at the back border. This is afterwards sewn up and completed. With a foam cushion the unit is inserted in the cover straightway and the cover opening sewn up.

CHAPTER XVI

TELEVISION CHAIR

THE design illustrated in Fig. 1 is contemporary in both its styling and build. Quebec birch or a good beech are still the best timbers for upholstery frames, but may not be easy to obtain. If not available use close-grained timber that is unlikely to split.

FIG. I.   A COMFORTABLE CHAIR ON CONTEMPORARY LINES.

Framework. Mark out the rails, cut, and clean to size. The seat and back side rails are rounded on the top edges excepting the 3½ in. left square on the rear end of the seat rails to take the back uprights. These latter two uprights can either be grooved or bored to take the tension springs. Boring separate sockets the diameter of the springs as in Fig. 2 is probably the neatest way of fixing the back springs. The seat springs are fixed to the back and front seat rails. Therefore these too must be either bored or grooved. Grooves are favoured here as they are practically unseen.

GROOVE FOR
SPRINGS

18¼"

FIG. 2. FRAMEWORK.
Note that the spring sockets in the back uprights are not taken
right through.

The side seat rails and back uprights are dowelled together using three dowels for each joint. As it will have to take a good deal of strain, cut the angle on the back uprights accurately, use a good glue and cramp hard to ensure a sound joint. Allow ample time to thoroughly set. When these sections are ready they can be linked together with the cross rails, i.e., the seat back and front rails and back tacking rail. Leave the top back rail till last. This is a 1½ in. bowed rail which is cut and lightly housed in the back uprights before gluing and screwing.

The legs are cut to shape, cleaned, and half-lapped onto the side, front and back rails. When they are glued and screwed in position they also act as corner braces.

Polishing. Well sand the visible parts before staining all over to shade required. Rub in some filler on the front edges and start the polishing. This can be by the older method of using button polish and building up first by brushing on, afterwards bodying up with a rubber. Rub down with a fine glass-paper between each application. If a spray gun is available the whole of the frame can be

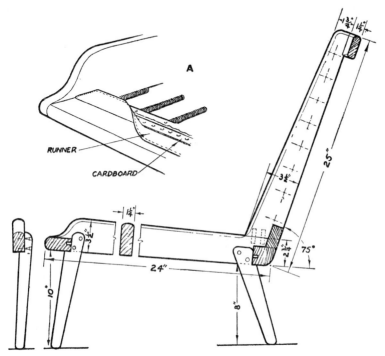

FIG. 3. THROUGH SECTION OF FRAME, WITH MAIN DIMENSIONS.
Note that the legs are half-lapped to the side rails. The slight outward splay ensures that the weight is directly on the foot. Detail (A) method of fixing the front seat runner.

sprayed and finished with a "pullover." This method requires thin cellulose and a cellulose "pullover." Alternatively a brushing cellulose could be used. This, too, is finished with a "pullover" for a good result.

A pullover is the trade name for a thin cellulose mixture used on a rubber. The rubber consists of a piece of wadding or cotton linters covered with a piece of clean washed rag. It is used both with french polish or with pullover. The wadding is soaked on its top surface with polish and the rag laid over so the polish works through the rag. In the case of french polish a finger-tip spot of neatsfoot oil is laid on the rag after it is pulled over the wadding.   This lubricates the rubber and prevents it from sticking.   The oil must *not* be used with a cellulose finish.

Before the polishing is completed, the back tension springs should be fixed so that any marks can be easily removed.   It does not matter with the seat springs so much as they are nailed from the top of the rails and covered with material.   Brassed or plated escutcheon pins are useful for fixing the springs as these are easier to remove should a spring require replacing.

Upholstery.   There is little complicated upholstery on this chair as a foamed latex cushion is suggested for the seat and a rubberised hair and linter's felt for the back, though foamed latex can be used here also.

Eight $\frac{1}{2}$ in. diameter tension springs are needed for the seat and three for the back plus five $\frac{3}{8}$ in. springs.   A first choice for the seat springs would be the braid-covered type and second choice the plastic-covered.   It is doubtful if the $\frac{3}{8}$ in. size will be obtainable in the covered type, but one of the larger-covered size can be used at the top and two at the bottom.   As the back cushion is not reversible this does not matter a great deal except for appearance or if they rust.

The seat cushion is reversible so the seat springs must be covered either individually with braid or plastic, or an apron laid over them. The apron can be made of a lining or a thick fabric hemmed along the two ends and slotted at each side to take the first and eighth spring.   The rest of the apron passes over the top of the other springs.

A piece of material $4\frac{1}{2}$ in. wide is cut from the covering fabric. Cut this the full width and divide into two 1 ft. 8 in. pieces, and make a small hem along one edge of each piece.   These runners, as they are called, are stretched across the front and back seat rails and back tacked to them so that the hems lie over the springs.

Cushions.   It is intended that a foamed latex cushion approximately 4 in. at the edges and flat or only slightly domed should be used for the seat.   The width should be 18 in. and 20 in. from front to back.   It can be covered in almost any fabric and the small designs much in favour at the present time are suitable.   Whether a large or small designed fabric is decided upon take the most prominent feature of the pattern for the centre motif.   Make this the centre of both the seat and back cushions.

The back cushion can be made up with a piece of rubberised hair wrapped in one or two layers of linter's felt.   If the linter's is a thick grade, one thickness will be enough as the cushion should finish approximately 2½ in. thick at the centre. Add another layer of felt on the front at the top and bottom thus making a slight swelling at these points.

Most covering fabrics are 48 to 50 in. wide so the two panels for the seat cushion will cut from the width. This also applies to the front of the back cushion and the outside back. Cut these pieces

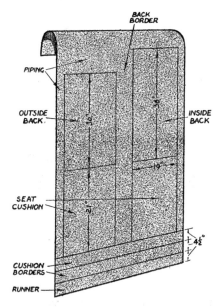

FIG. 4. SETTING OUT THE UPHOLSTERY.

only, leaving the strips in one length as these will be needed for the side borders of the back cushion. Allow ½ in. for sewing all round for the panels. The seat cushion borders should be cut rather tight, approximately 4½ in. to finish 3¾ in. on the piping. This will tighten up the cushion all round and give a clean finish. Cut the back cushion borders to the shape shown plus ½ in. sewing allowance all round. The back cushion is made up of a front panel, side borders, lining, and outside back. The front panel runs from the bottom of the side back borders, up and over the top of these to where it meets the first tension spring of the back. Here it is joined to the lining and the outside back.

A small hem is made on each side of the outside back and across the bottom edge.   Join the top edge of the outside back and the lining to the front panel first, then continue by joining the sides of the lining to the borders, thus making a bag of the front panel, the borders and lining, leaving the outside back loose on the sides and lower edge. Leave the bottom of the bag open to insert the felt-covered hair. When this is properly filled and evened out so there are no lumps or rucks the bottom is closed by slip-stitching.

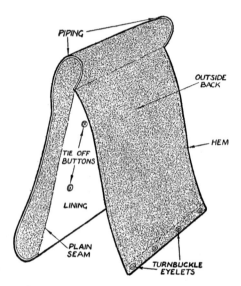

FIG. 5.   BACK CUSHION CONSTRUCTION.

Three buttons just below the top, and three above the bottom swellings will help to keep the shape of the cushion.   Space the buttons about 5 in. apart and tie in with a twine run through, using a mattress needle.   Use either matching or contrasting buttons on the front but any odd buttons will suffice at the back as these are only to stop the twine pulling through when the slip knot is pulled tight and knotted.

The back cushion rests on the back tension springs and is held in position by bringing the outside back over the top tension spring and down to the underside of the bottom seat rail.   It can be tacked down here, but the cushion itself can be made easily removable by fitting four eyelets on the bottom hem of the outside back and four turn buckles on the bottom rail.

CUTTING LIST

	Long ft. in.	Wide in.	Thick in.
2 Legs	1 0½	2	1¼
2 Legs	0 11½	2	1¼
2 Side pieces	2 1	4	1¼
2 Back pieces	2 0	4	1¼
1 Seat rail	1 7	3	1¼
1 Ditto	1 7	2½	2
1 Back rail	1 9¼	2½	1½
1 Stretcher	1 7	2½	1¼

Allowance has been made in lengths and widths. Thicknesses are net. In addition to the above are required eleven ½-in. tension springs; five ⅜-in. tension springs; foam rubber cushion 20 in. by 18 in. by 4 in. rubberised hair and linter's felt; 2 yards of 48 or 50 in. material and ¾ yard lining.

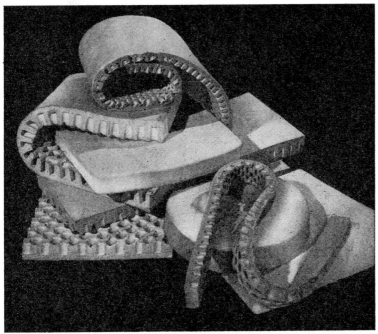

[Photograph by courtesy Liverpool Latex Cushion Co. Ltd., Liverpool.

LATEX FOAM MATERIALS USED IN UPHOLSTERY.

CHAPTER XVII

CONTEMPORARY WING EASY CHAIR

THE clean curves of contemporary furniture have much to recommend them as they lend themselves to the modern components of foamed latex and tension springing. Also, easy chairs

FIG. I. MODERN VERSION OF THE WING EASY CHAIR.
Upholstered in contrasting colours, it gives a most pleasing appearance.

with wings give just that extra comfort and protection from draughts that is so much appreciated. Both these factors have been incorporated in this design.

Choosing a cover. A contemporary divan, chair, or settee requires a contemporary cover, but if it is desired to use the chair with more conventional furniture choose one of the quieter designs or a plain cover. The fabric can be a cotton or wool moquette, cotton or wool tapestry, or one of the mixed yarn fabrics decorated with stripes, dots, flecks, or small sprays of flowers. Four and a quarter yards of 50-in. material will be sufficient to cover.

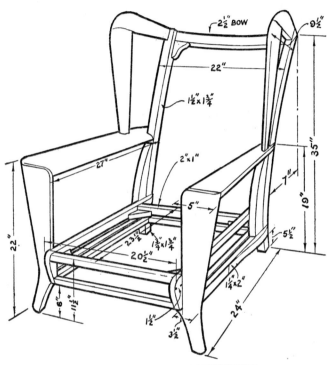

FIG. 2. DETAILS OF THE FRAMEWORK.

Measurements and shapes can be altered to blend with existing furniture. Here the seat frame is made as a separate unit and screwed within the main frame. If it is intended to build the whole as a complete unit the bottom seat rail is dowelled directly into the arm uprights, and the remaining sections fitted later. Mixed hardwoods can be used but should be of sound, straight-grained stuff.

Frame construction. The frame requires a sound, close-grained hardwood (preferably Quebec birch or Yugoslav beech); but many other timbers can be, and are often used. Ash, beech, chestnut, maple, and oak off-cuts are all reliable. Dowelled joints are used to join the sections together and is standard practice on most uphol-

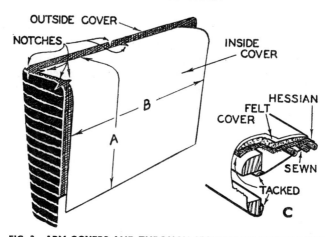

FIG. 3. ARM COVERS AND THROUGH SECTION OF FRONT RAILS.

The front rail covering is tacked to the underside or back of the top front rail, whichever is the easier.

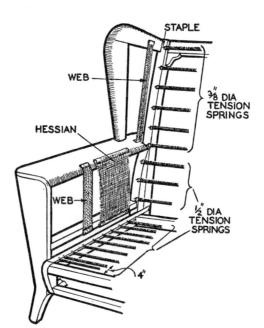

FIG. 4. SPRINGING THE FRAME.

The seat spring loops are fixed into a slot; the back springs stapled to the frame. Runners are laid over the seat spring ends to prevent chafing.

stered frames.   A good glue should be used and all joints cramped as tightly as possible during assembly.   If the curved rails are band-sawn they will need some cleaning up after cutting.

Assembly.   The front rail, arm uprights, and back framing can be made up first, using three dowels for the seat rails, and two for the top back rail.   When prepared join the sections with the side and arm rails, adding the wings last.

The inner seat frame can be made up and fitted after the main frame is assembled, but before doing this the method of fixing the springs should be decided upon.   An 18- or 20-gauge metal plate punched for nine springs and screwed or nailed on is one way. Another is to make a narrow groove about $\frac{3}{8}$ in. wide along the insides of the rails as in Fig. 4, or to bore holes in the same position at 2 in. spacings.   With either of these last two methods the fixing is made by placing the end of the spring in the slot or hole and driving a nail through top rail to catch the spring loop.

A light tacking rail for the arm covers is fixed an inch above the springing rails with a single dowel at the front, the rear end being housed and screwed into the back upright.   Four brackets are glued and screwed in the corners of the seat rails to offset the pull of the springs.   On completion the stumps or legs, the spring rails, and all woodwork not covered by upholstery should be stained and polished as required.

Cutting the cover (arms).   Using a tape, measure the inside of the arm from the spring rail to the top outer edge, allowing $1\frac{1}{2}$ in. for turning, Fig. 3 (A).   The width is taken from the inside of the arm upright to the back upright as in Fig. 3 (B).   The outside arm measurements are made to meet the inside arm.   These pieces are cut out and fixed in position with a few temporary tacks.   A chalk line along the front and top edge is made and trimmed off to within $\frac{1}{2}$ in.   The outside cover is offered up and the operation repeated. When the two are together make a meeting notch on each at the two top corners of the arm upright as indicated in Fig. 3.   Having checked for accuracy they are removed from the frame and used as templates for the other arm.   Join the sections by machining together with piping inserted between each, taking care that the notches come together.

Front edge.   This is brought from the top seat rail over the second spring to the front rail and thence to the underside of the bottom seat rail as shown in Fig. 3 (C).   A piece of hessian sewn on the wrong side of the cover along the position occupied by the second spring and long enough to reach to the top seat rail over the front spring, reduces excessive wear on the cover when in use.   Two strips or runners approximately 4 in. wide are cut and a ½-in. hem made along one side.

Having cut and sewn the above cover pieces the upholstery can be started. First tack two pieces of web on each arm tacking rail and strain them to the top arm rails. Next, tack a piece of hessian on each arm over the webs, starting along the tacking rail and pulling taut to the top rail, also on the arm upright.

Double over the hessian and webs when tacking on, and turn over the raw edge after tacking off on the top rails. Use ½-in. improved tacks on the webs, and ½-in. or ⅜-in. improved on the hessian.

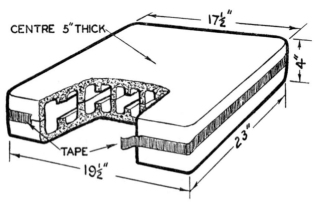

FIG. 5. LATEX FOAM CUSHION.
This is usually made by joining two moulded shapes together with solution and taping the seams.

The seat springing. These should be ½-in. diameter tension springs preferably covered with braided cotton or plastic. Plain steel springs can be used but will require a lining apron fitted over the main body of springs to prevent damaging the cover.

The runners or strips are tacked along the outer edges of the spring rails so as to cover the rails and lie over the ends of the springs. With fabric or plastic covered springs this is all that is needed. If an apron is required a piece of lining is hemmed all round with the back and front hems left open so that the third front, and last spring can be inserted. This lining rests over the middle springs.

Covering (front edge). Start by tacking the back edge of the cover to the top seat rail on the top edge passing over the first spring and under the second spring. Follow the cover with a piece of hessian under-and-over the second spring and tack down along the top of the top seat rail. Lay a thickness of linter's felt on the hessian, bring the cover over, and tack down to the underside of the bottom seat rail. The latter is first fixed with temporary tacks as the surplus on the ends will need easing out and possibly folding on the top near the arm uprights.

Arms. Here the stuffing can be simply two layers of linter's felt, or a thin layer of fibre and a layer of linter's. A better stuffing is a piece of rubberised hair cut to fit the top arm rail and eased off at the edge where it meets the linter's on the inside of the arm, the whole being covered with a layer of linter's felt. Although often omitted, the outer arm covering can be lined with a light hessian to give it a backing. This is tacked to the top rail and front upright but left hanging at the back and bottom until the final tacking off.

The cover should be laid over without disturbing the stuffing and pulled into position gradually. Clean out any fullness and pull the piping taut before temporarily tacking down the bottom of the inside arm to the back of the spring rail. Temporarily tack the rest of the cover and proceed with springing the back. Six $\frac{3}{8}$-in. tension springs are fixed above the arms and three of the stronger $\frac{1}{2}$-in. size below. These springs can be stapled to the back uprights as in Fig. 4. Stuffing for the back can be carried out with a fibre pad, that is, fibre woven on hessian. This should be slightly larger than the back and tacked on loosely all round, particularly from side to side. Another method is to make up a hessian bag, again oversized, filled with fibre, hair, or kapok. Run this through prior to fixing with a few twine ties to hold the filling in place. Over this is laid a good layer of linter's felt. Measurements for the inside back cover are taken from the underside of the lower back rail to the outside of the top back rail. The required sizes are cut and placed in position, and temporarily fixed all round with $\frac{1}{2}$-in. fine tacks. Clean out all fullness and pull fairly taut from bottom to top. Tension should not be so great from side to side, but clear of all rucks and fullness. Finally tack down to the front of the back uprights, the back of the top back rail, and the underside of the lower back rail. All raw edges are left except for the bottom rail, where it is turned in.

Buttoning the back. Mark out with chalk dots half diamonds for the buttons approximately $5\frac{1}{2}$ in. wide and $3\frac{1}{2}$ in. up. The buttons are "floated" in, using a fine strong twine and mattress needle, tying with a slip knot pulled tight to the hessian and secured by a knot above the slip knot.

Covering the wings. Back tacking the wing covering on the top arm rail requires good judgment, and possibly it would be better to web and hessian first. To do this a piece of web is folded in half and tacked on the top of the arm rail close to the back upright, straining

9—P.U.

it tightly to the top wing rail (see Fig. 4). A piece of hessian large enough to cover the front of the wing is tacked to the wing rails, and with one or two tacks to the arm rail against the web. Follow the line of the web with a folded edge of the hessian and pull taut, and make a series of running twine stitches to hold the hessian to the web. Measure over the wing for the cover and cut a pair of inside and outside pieces.

The inside cover is tacked to the top arm rail on the wrong side, so that the major part falls down over the arm. Two good layers of linter's felt are placed on the hessian and the cover pulled upwards to the top wing rail. Here and round the wing upright it is fixed with several temporary tacks. The back edge is pulled past the web to the back upright. Clean out fullness and tack off all round with $\frac{3}{8}$-in. or $\frac{1}{2}$-in. fine tacks. Complete both wings.

Finishing off. A piece of piping is made up and tacked across the top of the back and around the wing edges. The wing outer faces are covered and should be lined with a piece of hessian, especially if a thin cover is used. A half thickness of linter's laid on the hessian makes a good finish. When fixing the outside wings tack close to the piping with a few temporary tacks. The outside arm covers are brought across the lower part of the wings, the piping pulled taut, and fixed temporarily. The bottom edges are turned in and tacked off, the back edges being tacked to the back uprights.

Tack and strain a web from the centre of the top rail to the bottom rail. The back outer covering is placed over this and back tacked along the top back rail close to the piping. Again a light hessian lining will make a better finish, although this is not absolutely vital. The cover is pulled taut to the bottom rail, the edge turned under and tacked off on the underside. Turn in the side edges and fix temporarily. Finish off by slip-stitching these edges and wings.

The cushion. This can be of foamed latex, polyether foam, or the spring interior type. Most of the latex firms make a standard size cushion which will fit this chair.

Foamed latex. Lay the uncovered cushion on the seat and cut a paper pattern to fit. Using the pattern as a template, cut the top and bottom pieces for the cushion, allowing for seams. The borders should be cut $4\frac{1}{2}$ in. to finish approximately $3\frac{3}{4}$ in., thus making a tight cover. When joining the sections pipe all round the seams.

Spring interior. This is built up on the open mesh principle or with pocketed springs and layers of linter's felt. The open mesh unit is covered with hessian or fibre on hessian pad. Two layers of linter's felt are wrapped round it, the whole being compressed and inserted into the case. The case is made up the same manner as for the rubber cushion. A much larger opening, however, must be left to take the spring. Usually, the full width of the back and along the sides for 8 or 9 in. is needed. When the spring is finally housed the opening is closed with neat slip-stitching, using stout carpet thread.

To complete the chair domes are fitted to the bottoms of the stumps.

[Photographs by courtesy of Liverpool Latex Cushion Co. Ltd.

EXAMPLES OF LATEX FOAM CUSHIONS.

These can be obtained in many shapes and sizes, and either uncovered or covered with tapestry, moquette, repp, etc.

CHAPTER XVIII

THREE-PIECE SUITE

THE suite illustrated in Fig. 1 is a fairly simple, modern design lending itself to almost any soft covering. It would be rather more difficult in leathercloth or hide. A slightly different build-up of the seat would be needed, as cushion seats are advisable. The sizes given are suitable for the average size room. If required for a large room the appearance could be made bolder by increasing the over-all length of the settee. A plump person might require an inch or so extra between the arms of the chairs, but the sizes are suitable for general use.

FIG. I. COMFORTABLE FULLY UPHOLSTERED SETTEE AND ARMCHAIRS.

A soft cover is suggested for these items. Hide or leathercloth would be more difficult and would need a rather different build-up.

CHAIR

Starting with the chair the first item is the frame. Birch, beech, ash, maple, and oak in the order named are the choice of woods for preference. A close-grained hardwood capable of taking tacks without splitting and holding dowelled joints is the ideal.

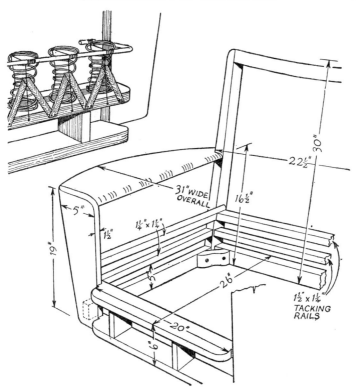

FIG. 2. DETAILS AND SIZES OF THE CHAIR FRAME.

After setting out and cutting to size the various rails, assemble the arm. Use good glue and cramp tightly. Join up with the seat and back rails, and fix the corner blocks with glue and screws. A $\frac{3}{8}$-in. hole is bored in the centre of each corner block to receive the castors. The last-named can be the detachable, generally called "push in" type. Fig. 2 shows the frame.

Webbing. The frame completed, turn it upside-down, resting the seat rail on a trestle or bench corner, and start webbing. Six strands of good-quality web are required from front to back and five from side to side. Work from the front rail first, tacking on the web by folding over about an inch and using $\frac{5}{8}$-in. improved tacks or clout nails. Space the strands about $1\frac{3}{4}$ in. apart, straining each one tightly with a web strainer. Tack down with four $\frac{5}{8}$-in. tacks through the single thickness of web, cutting off about 1 in. beyond the tacks. Turn over this end and fix with two tacks. The side-to-side webs are alternately checked under and over the others. Having completed the webbing of the seat place the chair upright on trestles or bench. The arms are webbed and hessianed next. Fig. 3 gives webbing.

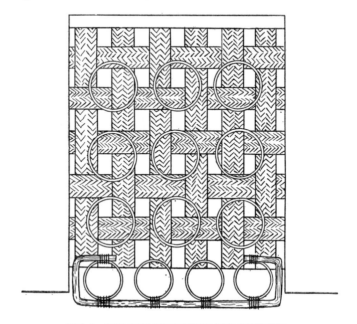

FIG. 3. LAY-OUT OF SPRINGS AND WEBBING.

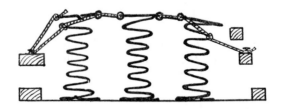

FIG. 4. LACING OF THE SEAT SPRINGS FROM BACK TO FRONT.

Two webs are needed up and down on each inside arm and one on the outside; $\frac{1}{2}$-in. improved tacks will be most suitable for this webbing and the hessian. The hessian is tacked on the inside arms all round, starting at the bottom tacking rail with a turned over edge and pulling taut to the top arm rail. Do the same from back to front.

The outside arm hessian is tacked on the top arm rail first and part of the way down both back and front uprights. When this is done fold the loose end over the web out of the way. It will not be finally tacked on the bottom rail until a later stage.

The springing. Springing the seat is the next operation; six 10-in. by 8-gauge, three 9-in. by 8-gauge, and four 5- or 6-in. by 10-gauge springs are required. The 9-in. springs form the back row and the 10-in. the middle and front rows. The position of the front row of springs is governed by the 5- or 6-in. springs to be used on the front edge.

Hold one of the 5- or 6-in. springs on the front rail and set the first row of 10-in. springs about 1 in. behind the top rung of this spring. The back row of 9-in. springs is placed slightly in front of the back tacking rail, whilst the middle row is set midway between the front and back rows (see Fig. 3). Sew the springs to the web with three ties to each spring, the ties starting with a slip-knot and the twine being kept taut between each tie. Tack a piece of hessian or odd soft material on the front rail as an anti-knock for the springs.

Lacing the tops of the springs in position with a stout non-stretch cord is the next item. Cut three pieces of laid cord, each to pass from the seat, back tacking rail, over the springs to the front rail, and returning to the top rung of the first spring; also allow for the ties. Fix a cord by tying round a tack on the seat tacking rail opposite each row of springs. Bring one of the cords to the second rung of a back spring, tie or half-hitch around the coil, and pass to the top rung. Carry on to the middle and front springs, tying on both sides of the top coil of the middle spring and one side of the top coil of the front spring. Bring the cord down to the second or third coil of the front spring. Pull taut round a tack on the front rail, but before driving the tack home make sure the springs are in their proper positions.

The back spring should lean a trifle outwards, the centre one very slightly forward and the front one rather more forward (see Fig. 4). When satisfied with the positions of the springs knock the tack home and return the surplus cord to the top rung of the front spring. Repeat over each row of springs from back to front, then from side to side.

The edge springing. The front edge springs are stapled to the front rail. Four in number, the two end ones are about ¾ in. from the arms, and the other two equally spaced. Cut a piece of web in half and tack one end on the front of the front rail. Pass the other end up and through a lower middle rung of the first spring, returning to the rail again and pulling the spring well forward before tacking down. Repeat with each spring. Next cut four pieces of laid cord long enough to pass from the rail over the spring and back to the rail. Tie one of these cords at the back of the bottom rung of a spring. Bring the cord to the middle rung and tie again, pulling the spring into an upright position. Carry on to the top rung and tie again, then to the second rung downwards, and so to the front edge of the spring rail. Repeat with each spring, tacking down the cords so that the top coils are approximately level with the front 10-in. springs of the seat. The edge springs should finish upright in position.

The actual edge is formed by lashing a piece of cane or wire along the front edges of the top rungs of the edge springs. Use cane for preference about the thickness of the little finger. An 8-gauge wire or an old spring unwound and knocked out can be used. Bend each end round to form a return the size of the top coil of an edge spring. Lay the cane or wire on the edge springs and, using thin twine, whip the cane to the front edge of the top coil of each spring; also the returns to the back edge of the end springs. (See detail in Fig. 3.)

The whole of the springing is covered with a heavy quality hessian. This hessian is tucked down between the front edge springs and the main springs to form a gutter or valley. Fix all round with temporary tacks except at the front. The gutter is held in place by a series of laid cord loops passing through the hessian and back to the front rail before being tacked down between the springs. The front portion of the spring hessian is brought over the springs and on to both front seat rails. Tack off the hessian all round with $\frac{3}{8}$-in. or $\frac{1}{2}$-in. improved tacks for preference. The tops of the springs are sewn to the hessian with three ties, using the same method as when sewing to the webs. The cane is also bound to the hessian with a series of half-hitches spaced about $1\frac{1}{2}$ in. apart. Finally, two loose loops of twine are made across the top of the front edge.

First stuffing—the seat. These loops are to take the first stuffing, the next operation. Coco fibre (or " ginger " fibre, as it is commonly called) is most suitable unless horsehair is available. Pack a fairly firm, even amount along the sides and back of the seat and under the loops on the front edge. Fill the gutter firmly, preferably with flock unless hair is being used. Fibre or flock can be used over the centre portion of the seat, just sufficient to avoid feeling the springs through.

Cover the stuffing with a piece of scrim or light hessian, securing it at the front with three or four skewers. Make a square of running-through ties in the centre of the seat, avoiding the gutter. Pick over the front edge fibre and even out to form a compact firm edge.

Refix the scrim in place with skewers, turning in the edge of the scrim. This edge is sewn to the hessian at the cane. A sink or blind stitch is also made across the front at this same point. Regulate the stuffing well forward with a regulator or stout needle.

Complete the edge with a top stitch to form a roll about the size of a thumb. Both kinds of stitches are started with slip-knots. Continue by inserting the needle about 1½ in. ahead each time then returning it half-way behind the point of insertion. With the blind stitch the needle is returned before pulling clear of the scrim on the top of the edge. The twine is twisted round the needle as it is withdrawn and pulled taut. Turn in the edges of the scrim along the sides and back and tack down. This completes the seat for the present so the back can be dealt with next.

The back. The webbing of the back consists of three webs up and down and four webs crosswise. All are tacked to the outer edges

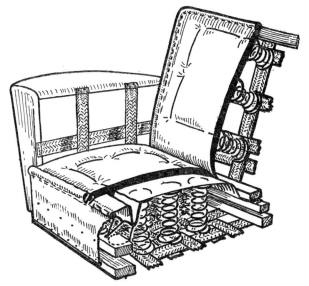

FIG. 5. CUT-AWAY VIEW OF SEAT AND BACK SHOWING FIRST STUFFING.

of the back uprights and rails with ⅝-in. improved tacks. Six 6-in. by 12-gauge springs are positioned on the crossing points of the top and middle webs and three 6-in. by 10-gauge on the bottom two webs. They are sewn to the webs in the usual manner, but are not fully laced as in the seat. The top springs are pulled upwards by passing a piece of laid cord round the second or third rung of each spring and fixed with tacks to the top rail. The middle and bottom springs can be laced through their middle rungs from side to side. This will keep them in place whilst covering with hessian, which is the next operation. Tack down the hessian on the front edge of the rails, doubling over the edges. The tops of the springs are sewn to the hessian with three ties to each. Make several loops of twine on the hessian about 2 in. inwards from the side and top rails. Pick an even quantity of fibre under these twines and fill in the bottom and centre. Lay a piece of scrim or light hessian over the stuffing and fix in place with a few temporary tacks.

A square of running-through ties similar to the seat are made in the centre of the back. After running through, the scrim is tacked down all round. Aim at a fairly firm, even edge along the top and sides with a slight swell at the bottom of the back. Form a roll round the back from the top of one arm to the other by making a "sink" or "blind" stitch all round. This completes the first stuffing of the chair, and, although it is not seen, it is the vital part upon which the durability and comfort of the job is based.

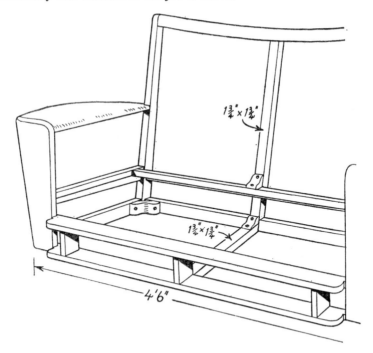

FIG. 6. SETTEE FRAMEWORK SHOWING CONSTRUCTION.
Sizes and timber dimensions are the same as those of the chair frame except the over-all width and stretcher rails.

SETTEE

Having dealt with the webbing, springing, and first stuffing of the easy chairs, we now pass to the settee, since it is generally more economical to plan and cut the cover for the complete suite. The settee is constructed on similar lines to the easies. Apart from minor adjustments, the frame is an enlarged edition of the chair frame. The dimensions of the rails and the width of the arms are the same as for the chairs unless an extra large settee is required. If this is desired extend the width and use two stretcher rails on seat and back equally spaced; also it is advisable to use a heavier front seat rail. Settee sizes can vary from 4 ft. to 6 ft. 6 in. over-all. The size dealt with in this article is 4 ft. 6 in. over-all. It is suitable for most modern rooms and seats two persons comfortably.

The frame is set out, dowelled and assembled in the same way as the chair frame, but note the stretcher rails in the seat and back. These are essential and must be neatly fitted and dowelled in position. Corner blocks glued and screwed to the rails will help the rigidity of the frame and also provide a suitable place for fitting the castors. Details are given in Fig. 6.

Webbing the seat. The first upholstery operation is webbing the seat. Five long webs are required, and these are tacked on first. Start tacking on the left side of the frame as it is turned upside down (viewed from the front). Strain tightly to the right-hand rail and tack down. Follow the same methods as with the webbing of the chair, using ⅝-in. improved tacks, and check the front to back webs under and over. The short webs are tacked on the front rail and strained to the back rail. Work from the centre stretcher rail, placing the first web on each side close to this rail. Space the following webs about 1¾ in. apart. Six good-quality webs each side, on a 4 ft. 6 in. settee should be sufficient, with other sizes in proportion. Fig. 7 shows the webbing from the rear.

When the webbing is completed, fold a piece of web in half and tack it across the stretcher rail with two tacks in each space between the long webs. This gives additional support to the webbing at the centre of the seat. The frame is now stood upright on trestles or a similar suitable working base.

Webbing the arms is the next item. Two up and down on each inside arm, and one on each outside arm are required. The hessian is tacked on in a similar manner to the chair arms, fully covering the inside arms and half covering the outside arms at this stage.

The springing of the seat. There are eighteen springs in the body

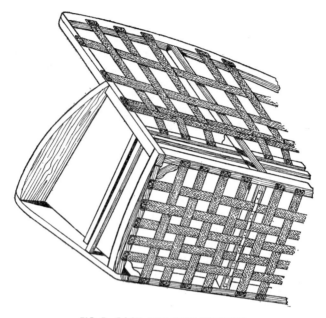

FIG. 7. BACK AND SEAT WEBBING.

Note the method of supporting the long webs at the stretcher rails. It is not always possible to check the back webbing completely, but endeavour to obtain a flat, true base for the springs.

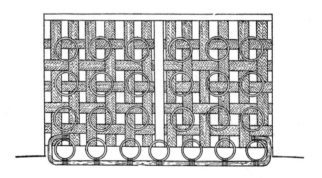

FIG. 8. LAY-OUT OF SEAT SPRINGS AND WEBBING.

of the seat and seven on the front rail (see Fig. 8). The eighteen consist of the two rows of 10-in. by 8-gauge, and one row of 9-in. by 8-gauge. Set up the springs in three rows from back to front approximately the same as in the chair. The six rows across the seat are arranged with a row each side of the stretcher rail, a row about 1½ in. from each inside arm, and middle rows between the two. The usual three-tie method is used for sewing the springs to the webs. Generally the most convenient starting-point for sewing the springs is from the left side of the front row. It is a matter of personal choice, however, whether the front or back row is dealt with first. With the springs all securely sewn to the web the lacing is next, and is an important item. Tack a strip of hessian on the front spring rail. This stops the edge springs from making a noise if one of the rungs hits the rail.

Cut six lengths of laid cord and fix one opposite each row of springs on the back tacking rail. Commence lacing from back to front, bringing the cord to the second rung of the back spring, tying there before passing to the top rung of the same spring. Tie again and continue to the top rung of the middle spring, and tie on both sides. Carry on to the top rung of the front spring and tie on one side, coming down to the second or third rung before tying again. Pull taut to a tack on the front rail. Make sure the springs are correctly positioned before tacking down. Repeat this operation with each row, pulling down each cord to the same degree so that all the tops of the springs are level.

The lengthwise lacings are started from the left side tacking rail. Leave a piece of cord for a return on each tack. Bring the long end of cord to the second or third rung of the first spring then to the top rung. Tie or half-hitch in the usual way and continue over all the springs on the top rungs until the last row. On this row repeat the starting procedure and pull taut to a tack on the tacking rail. The position of the springs should be upright except for the rows nearest the arms. These should lean outwards, that is, to the arms. Ascertain that the positions are correct before bringing the short ends of cord or returns to the top rungs of the end springs.

When the lacing is completed the tops of the springs should form a slight curve from arm to arm. From back to front there should be rather more of a curve with its lowest point at the back. Aim at an even surface, i.e. no one row or spring being higher or lower other than the normal curve.

Front edge springing. The front edge springs is the next item, and the methods employed are the same as on the chair front (see Fig. 3). This time seven springs are required instead of four. Place the springs one at each end, one in the middle and the others equally spaced between them. They will be almost between the rows of the main body springs, but it may be necessary to adjust one or two of the laid cord fixing tacks in order to place the edge spring in position. Pull the edge springs over with a web and tie back with laid cord as on the chair. A piece of cane or 8-gauge wire is bent to the required size, that is about $\frac{1}{2}$ in. from the arm uprights at each end. Whip the cane or wire to the front edge of the top coil of each spring and the returns to the back edges of the end springs.

This completed, cover the whole seat with a stout hessian, tucking

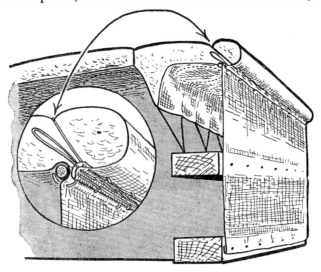

Fig. 9. SECTIONAL VIEW THROUGH THE SEAT.
The springs are omitted for clearness. This shows how the gutter is formed with the hessian, and the stitches used in making the roll or edge.

it down between the front edge springs and the front row of the body springs to form a gutter. Fix this at each end with a tack, pulling the hessian taut. Temporarily fix the remainder of the hessian at the back and sides. Tie the gutter in place with loops of laid cord through the hessian and back to tacks on the spring rail between the springs (see Fig. 9). The front portion of the hessian can then be tacked in place. Tack off on the bottom seat rail doubling under the edge, and afterwards add a few sparsely spaced tacks through the hessian at the spring rail level. Complete tacking down the hessian round the sides and back, turning over the edges. The tops of the springs and the cane are sewn to the hessian with the usual ties and hitches.

Cut a piece of scrim or hessian to cover the seat and tuck this down

at the back. Fix with half a dozen temporary tacks and lay the surplus over the tacking rails out of the way. Fill in the sides and back
with fibre and the gutter with hair or flock. Make three or four
loops of twine along the top of the front edge hessian and pick an
even amount of fibre under them. Fill in the centre of the seat with
a thin layer of hair, flock, or fibre. Bring the scrim over and fix with
skewers under the cane edge. Tuck down at the sides under the
arms and temporarily fix. Make three lines of running-through ties
on the main part of the seat behind the gutter.

This completed, the stuffing of the edge can be picked over,
evened out, and the scrim fixed evenly along the cane with skewers.
A fine twine in a half-circular needle is used to sew the scrim to the
hessian along the cane. Using a regulator or stout, straight needle,
regulate the edge stuffing well forward and start stitching the roll or
edge. Use a sink stitch first, just along the top of the cane. This
pulls the stuffing forward in a firm mass. The edge or roll is completed by a top stitch made as close as possible to the sink stitch on
the underside of the scrim and coming through on the top of the seat
about 1½ in. from the edge. Use a regulator frequently to work the
stuffing forward, thus forming a firm even edge a little thicker than
a man's thumb. Finish the scrim stuffing by tacking down the scrim
round the sides and back keeping the stuffing even. Fig. 9 shows a
section through the roll.

First stuffing the back. The build-up of the settee back is
similar to the chair back. All the webbing is tacked on to the back
edges of the rails, three webs up and down in each division of the
back, six in all ; and four webs lengthwise, two close together at the
bottom of the back, one approximately 3 in. from the top rail and one
in the middle of the back. Check the webs as far as possible. Six
6-in. by 10-gauge springs are set up and sewn to the bottom webs.
Twelve 6-in. by 12-gauge springs are sewn to the middle and top
positions at the crossing of the webs.

The bottom and middle rows of springs can be held in position by
lightly lacing with cord through the centre rungs of each spring.
Use one cord only from side to side on each row. Pull the springs
of the top row slightly upwards by passing a cord round their middle
rungs. Fix to ⅝-in. improved tacks on the top rail. Cover the
springs with hessian, fixing it in position with temporary tacks before
finally tacking down on the front edge of the rails. The tops of the
springs are sewn to the hessian with three ties. Cut a piece of scrim
or light hessian large enough to cover the back and allowing for the
depth of the roll or edge and turnings. Tack a turned-in edge of the
scrim on the back tacking rail.

Assuming that the settee is lying on its back on the trestles, pull the scrim out of the way, lay it over the seat, and push a skewer or two through it to keep it there. Proceed with the stuffing of the back. Use fibre round the edges, picked evenly under the usual loops of twine, and fibre, hair, or flock in the centre of the back. Pull the scrim over and fix all round temporarily. Starting at one of the bottom corners complete an oblong with a line through its centre, of long and short running-through ties. These ties can be pulled down fairly tightly, but leave the final tightening until the tacking off and stitching is completed. This is the next operation, to tack off the scrim evenly along the top and two sides of the back. The edge should be a little over 2 in. deep before stitching, evenly stuffed but not packed hard with fibre. If it is intended to use hair as the top stuffing a single sink or blind stitch is all that is required. Flock or fibre top stuffing loses its shape more quickly and it would be better to make a small top stitch as well.

Second stuffing. The settee and the two easies completed to the first or scrim stuffing stage, the planning and cutting of the covers can be proceeded with. In the pre-austerity days it was advisable to measure twice before cutting once. It is even more necessary with the present high prices. Double-width material, as it is termed, cuts more economically than single width. It may measure from 47 in. to 52 in. wide. Thirty-one inch, generally called single-width, or 36-in. materials will need more yardage and more joins. Large patterns and stripes often cut awkwardly and require more material.

All patterns, large or small, should be centred on the seat and back and balanced on the arms. This means trying to cut the two inside and two outside arms so they make a uniform pair. Endeavour to carry out these methods throughout the suite so that a symmetrical effect is obtained. The tops of the arms are piped on the outside edge, and the backs are piped along the top, outer edges, and down each side. The seat borders have two rows of piping, thus forming double borders. The seat is fitted and the two borders and piping are all machine stitched together.

Piping is made up by cutting strips of cover about $1\frac{1}{8}$–$1\frac{1}{4}$ in. wide. The strips are joined together, then folded over with a piping cord or laid cord inserted, and sewn together. Whenever possible cut the piping on the bias as it sets better when sewn. Piping cuts into a lot of material, so save all trimmings and odd pieces. Notes on this are given in Chapter VII.

Cutting the cover. Approximately $12\frac{1}{2}$ yards of 50-in. material will be required for the suite if made to the original sizes. The suggested layout of the cover in Fig. 10 is intended as a guide. It does not follow that any particular piece must be cut first. The pattern of the cover and how it will lend itself to the cutting sizes decides the order of cutting. Check the sizes given by measuring with a tape-measure over the actual job. The "inside" covers are all flyed. This term means that a piece of hessian or inexpensive material is sewn to the cover along the sides where it is not seen when pushed through between the arms and seat, or back and seat. The flys are

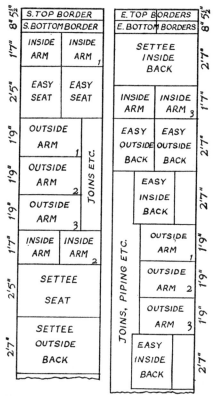

FIG. 10. SUGGESTED LAY-OUT OF THE COVER.
Note how the arm pieces are cut to pair, and are numbered to avoid mistakes.

really extensions of the main cover and are used for tacking down in the unseen positions. An example of how the cover can be flyed is given in Fig. 11.

Fitted parts. After cutting the cover the next operation is to cut the fitted parts. Starting with the arms, take an outside arm piece

10—P.U.

and fix it in place on one of the arms with a few temporary tacks.
Mark round this cover with chalk.   Cut a small notch with the
scissors in the material at the central point on the round where the
top arm and front upright meet.   Next place an inside arm piece in
position and notch this at the same point.   Remove both pieces and
cut the outside arm to the chalked shape plus a sewing allowance of
$\frac{3}{8}$–$\frac{1}{2}$ in.   Do not cut out the notch.

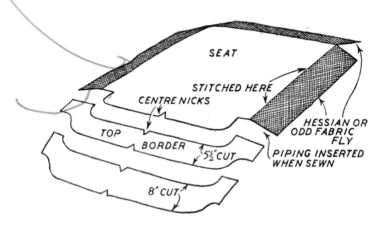

FIG. 11.   HOW SEAT COVER IS FLYED.   SEE ALSO SIDE JOINS.
The notches show the centre when cover is being worked into position.

The remaining outside arms and inside arms can be cut by using
this fitted outside arm as a template.   Cut in pairs, and number each
pair with chalk.   Notch the inside arms the same as the outsides.
This is shown in Fig. 12.

The inside arms are cut from the half-width, therefore requiring a
small join on the back edge.   A small facing-up piece may be needed
on the bottom front edge.   This is joined to the fly which is sewn on
the bottom edge.   When all the arms are cut and flyed the two
sections, inside and outside arms, can be sewn together with a piece
of piping inserted between.   The inside backs are also fitted on the
job.   Fix one in position with a few skewers, mark round it, remove
and cut to within $\frac{1}{2}$ in. of the mark.   It is advisable to fly the bottom
of the backs before fitting.

The front edge is finished with a double border.   As the height
from the bottom edge of the seat rail to the roll edge should finish
about 11 in., the proportion of $4\frac{1}{2}$–$6\frac{1}{2}$ in. looks well.   Cut the top
piece fairly tight, about $5\frac{1}{2}$ in., and the bottom piece 8 in.   Sew a

piece of piping along the top edge of the top border, then join the
top and bottom together with piping inserted between.   The seat
cover is now joined to the borders along the piping on the top edge
of the top border.

Second stuffing.   The cutting and sewing of the cover completed,
the next item is the top or second stuffing.   Hair is the first choice,
and if not used all over at least use it on the seats.   Make three series
of loops of twine across the seat, equally spaced, with the first one
about 2½ in. from the edge.   Assuming it is the easy seat about to be

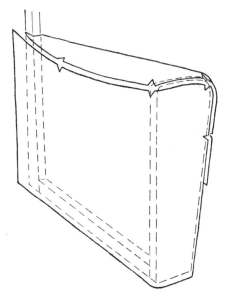

FIG. 12. HOW THE ARM COVER APPEARS WHEN THE
SECTIONS ARE CUT : ALSO WHEN THEY ARE ASSEMBLED.

covered (although it does not matter whether the chair or settee
comes first), take a seat cover and push the back fly through to the
back tacking rail.   Fix with three temporary tacks.   Lay the main
part of this cover on the inside back and fasten it there with a skewer.

Commence stuffing by lightly pushing small handfuls of hair along
the back of the seat.   Keep it even and open, not jammed in tightly.
Continue with small handfuls under the back row of twine.   Pick
over these handfuls and try to merge them into one as the stuffing
proceeds.   The hair should be opened out and loosely intermingled
with each preceding handful but not matted together in a hard mass.

From $1\frac{1}{2}$–2 lb. of hair, according to the grade, will be needed. Keep the shape of the seat to a gentle curve with the crown or apex a little forward of the centre.

Cover the hair with a layer of linter's felt or wadding. Pull the cover over and temporarily fix with three or four skewers along the front edge. Carefully push the side flys through to the side tacking rails and again fix temporarily. Keep the skewers temporarily in place along the front-edge until the seat cover is completely in position.

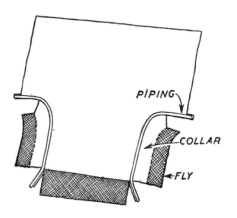

**FIG. 13. BACK COVER READY
TO PLACE IN POSITION.**

Make a parallel pencil or chalk mark along the spring hessian at $6\frac{1}{2}$ in. from the bottom edge of the seat rail. Place two thicknesses of linter's felt above this line under the top seat piping, remove the temporary skewers one or two at a time. Pull the top border over and down to the line on the hessian. Replace the skewers through the second piping. Get this straight along the line and sew it in place with a half circular needle and twine. This completed, tack down the side and back flys on the tacking rails.

Arms. The arms are the next item. As to the stuffing, hair and linter's felt or wadding, all linter's felt, or fibre and linter's felt can be used. Two layers of linter's felt on the inside and top arm and one layer on the outside is the easiest method. A layer of hair about 1 in. in depth picked on under twines and covered with wadding or felt makes a better job. It may be more difficult to get the cover over without displacing the stuffing but is worth the extra patience required.

The cover can be worked over from the front of the arm first, fixing at the back upright with two temporary tacks through the piping. Pull down the front portion next and fix in the same way. Clean the inside arm by tucking away the fly to the side tacking rail. When in the correct position tack down the bottom fly and the back fly. Repeat these operations on the other arm but leave the finishing off of the outside arms until later.

Back. Carry on with the back. Make the usual stringing-in loops, then tuck the back fly through to the back tacking rail. The best working position now is for the chair to be on its back on the trestles. Pick a fair thickness of hair under the twines, again keeping a nice rounded shape. Lay a piece of wadding or linter's felt over the hair and pull the cover over, fixing with a tack at each top. Place the chair on the floor, in which position the finishing can be done. Trim off the wadding or felt round the back border and pull the cover over, fixing it on the outside of the frame. Push the flys through and clean out rucks, etc. If the spare bottom ends of piping are tucked through under the arm tacking rails so that a pull is obtained to the side seat rails it will help to achieve a clean, tight finish. Tack off all round the back starting at the centre of the top, working along to the corners, then up from the arms to the corners. Finish the corners last with two neat pleats cleaned out as far as possible.

Front. Returning to the front of the chair (which can be turned on its back) where the bottom border is fixed in place a pencil or chalk line is made across the front at 6½ in. up from the bottom rail. The centre piece of piping is stretched across this mark and held with a tack at each end. Sew through the seam made by the borders and piping to the spring hessian. Two layers of linter's felt are placed on the hessian. The bottom portion of the cover is pulled over and tacked on the bottom of the seat rail and on to the two arm uprights.

Complete the tacking off of the outside arms next. Pull the hessian down and tack it on the seat rail, also on the back and front uprights. Push the linter's felt into place and pull the outside cover over, tacking down neatly and tautly all round including the front pipings. The small portion of arm piping crossing the bottom of the front border can be slip-stitched with thread.

Outside back. The outside back is dealt with next. Stretch a web from the centre of the bow to the seat rail. Then a piece of light hessian is tacked over the outside back as a lining first. Tack a piece of piping around the outline of the back and arms. There are several ways of fixing the outside back. Probably the best is to back-tack the top edge and fix the sides with temporary tacks, then slip-stitch with thread.   Alternative methods are to slip-stitch or gimp pin all round. The bottom edge is tacked on the underside of the seat rail.   A light hessian bottom over the webs provides the final touch.

Covering the settee is carried out on similar lines.   It is a larger job, but only requires a little more patience.

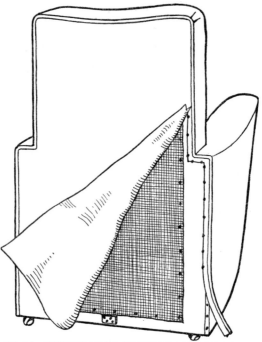

F'G. 14.   OUTSIDE BACK, SHOWING HESSIAN LINING, PIPING, ETC.

This completes a suite carried out by hand-sprung methods, the traditional way of upholstering for many, many years.   It is now decreasing in volume as mass-production methods increase and custom-built upholstery is enjoyed by the few.

CONTEMPORARY THREE-PIECE SUITE

(See page 154)

Fabric Cutting List

Use 50 in. wide material. Inside and outside measurements are given separately so that a two-colour scheme can be used. All sizes are approximate, and it is advisable to check against the actual job.

Inside arms, settee and easies . .	19 in. × half width
Inside back settee	33 in. × full width
,, ,, easy	33 in. × half width
Seat and border, settee . . .	14 in. × full width
,, ,, ,, easy . . .	14 in. × half width
Inside wings	17½ in. × 12 in.
Cushions, tops and bottoms . . .	21 in. × 21 in.
Cushion borders	4½ in. × full width
Outside arms and wings . . .	16 in. × 32 in.
	16 in. × 10 in.
Outside backs	32 in. × full width
	32 in. × half width

Piping from surplus from wings and widths plus ½ yard, making 9 yards for insides, and 4½ yards for outsides.

ATTRACTIVE CONTEMPORARY CHAIR WITH LOOSE CUSHION.

This is the *Andora* chair made by James Barrett Ltd.
Height of seat 17 in., depth of seat 23 in., height inside back 21 in.
Over-all height 32 in., over-all width 29 in.

CHAPTER XIX

CONTEMPORARY THREE-PIECE SUITE

DESPITE increasing mass-production methods in the manu-facture of upholstered furniture there is still a vast range of designs from which to choose one's particular style of comfort. The Nordic influence is still with us, although it merges into many designs all designated together under the "contemporary" label.

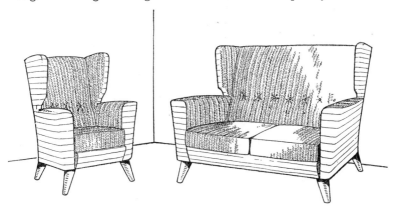

FIG. I. SIMPLE MODERN SUITE WITH LOOSE CUSHIONS.

The suite in Fig. 1 comes under this heading, and the materials suggested for its construction are also of the present age. Some were in limited use before the war, but all have come into general use since that period.

Frames. Close-grained, sound timber is required for the frames. North American birch used to be the most favoured wood, but is difficult to obtain now. A good beech is quite suitable, and other close-grained timbers are equally useful. Some of the newer timbers being introduced do not take tacks too well, several tacks in a line causing splits. Dowels $\frac{3}{8}$ in. diam. are used on all joints except those on the front ends of the seat-springing rails; mortise and tenon joints are recommended here. The arm uprights or facings, back uprights, and all side rails are the same sizes on both chairs and settee, the front and back rails making the difference in width between chairs and settee.

Cut the arm upheads and the front rail, bore for four-$\frac{3}{8}$ in. dowels in each end of the front seat rail. Also bore the backs of the upheads for the arm and side rails, and cut the mortises for the seat-springing rails. The settee side rails can be dowelled as the springing is from back to front. Use the same method with the back upheads, marking out and boring the dowel holes for both the back-cross rails and side rails. After this has been completed assemble the back framing.

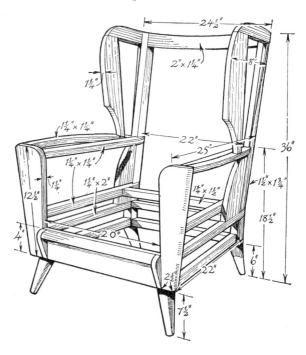

FIG. 2. SIZES AND DETAILS OF CHAIR FRAME.

When the glue on both the front and back sections has set, assemble the frame complete with the side rails, and add the pieces of the wing framing. Finally fit the front legs. These are rounded and tapered and also set at the slight angle as shown. Fix in position with $\frac{1}{4}$ in. bolts. Alternatively, ready-turned legs with various fixing devices can be bought for the front legs.

Note that the outer edges of all members which could chafe the upholstery fabric are rounded off.

Springing. It is suggested that the suite would look attractive covered in two contrasting colours such as black on the outsides, with red, off-white, yellow, or blue on the insides; or perhaps red and grey, green and beige, or a patterned cover on the insides. A plain one could be used on the outsides. Approx. 9 yards of 50 in. wide fabric are required for the insides and cushions, and 4½ yards for the outsides. Nine ½ in. diameter tension springs are used in each easy-chair seat (eighteen in the settee seat), and ⅜ in. diameter for

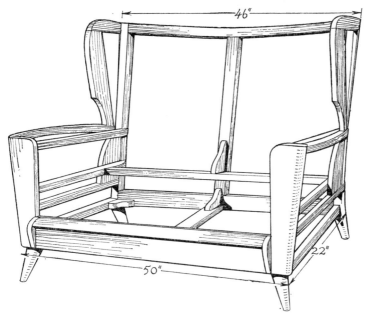

FIG. 3. SETTEE FRAME. SIZES OTHER THAN WIDTH AS CHAIR.

the backs. Before starting the upholstery mark out and cut to shape six pieces of plywood to fit the top of the arms, so that the straight edge rests on the top of the inside straight rail and the curved edge fits the underside of the outside rail: the ply is then glued and nailed on.

Arms. Now for the actual upholstery. Tack two webs on each arm, spacing the first about 10 in. from the front and the other near the back upright, one end being tacked on at the lower tacking rail and stretched to the top rail. Use ½ in. improved tacks for the webs and also for the hessian which is tacked on next over the webs. Strain both webs and hessian tightly when tacking off except at the back uprights, where it is left loose but long enough to tack down on the uprights later. The plywood-covered space on the top of the arms is filled in with some loose fibre or hair stuffing, and covered with the extending piece of hessian.

Fix the back springs in position using either of the methods shown to hold them in place. Use two ½ in. diameter springs on the lower part of the backs, four on the settee back. Fill in the top portions with the ⅜ in. springs spaced approximately 3 in. apart, keeping the top one as near the top as possible. Cover this springing with a fibre or hair pad, that is, hair or fibre woven on to hessian. Another method would be to use hessian over the springs and rubberized hair laid on the hessian. In either case hold it in place with a few tacks at the top and bottom rails.

Wings. The wings are webbed and hessianed in the same way as the arms, a web being stretched from the top arm rail to the top of the wing close to the back upright. Tack the hessian on the wing framing and pull the back edge through the space between the web and upright. Fix on to the uprights with three or four tacks, and make several ties with twine along the web to hold the hessian to it. This completed, the fixing tacks can be released so the space is open again. The loose edge of hessian will be tacked off later when the wing is covered. Unless the side seat rails have been grooved for rings as illustrated, use plates for fixing the seat springs. These are bored at 2 in. spacing for the springs and are screwed into a rebate on the top of the rails. Pirelli or similar rubber webbing can be used instead of springs and a lining would not be needed over the web. The chairs have now reached the stage when the cover can be cut and fitted, and the settee should be dealt with in a similar way.

Cutting the Cover. Present trends in covering fabrics tend to be of the plain type, or at least not set patterned, but there is no reason why a patterned material should not be used on the insides and a plain one on the outsides.

Before cutting a patterned material, plan the cover so that there is a centre pattern on the seat cushions and inside backs. Measure each section of the suite with a tape measure allowing ½ in. for all sewing edges and about an inch for turning under when tacking down. After cutting the inside and outside arms fix one of each on an arm with fixing tacks.

Cut each to shape to fit the arm, notching at several points, remove from the arm and cut the remaining five arms from these templates, not forgetting the notches or to pair the three sets of arms. Join up the inside and outside arms with a piping between them—the piping can be made up first using a 1½ in. strip of material with a piece of cord inserted. The centre portion of each seat can be covered with a lining starting about 6 in. inwards from the front edge. Allow the front cover to come from the first spring over the front rail down to the bottom rail, tacking off on the underside, and cut this front piece wide enough to tack off on the side rails.

Join to the lining leaving 6 in. of lining under the cover: this will come under No. 1 spring. Fix in place temporarily and cut the sides

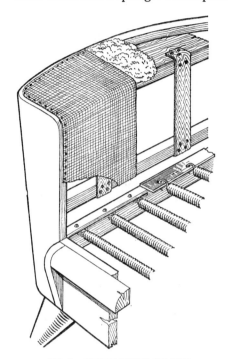

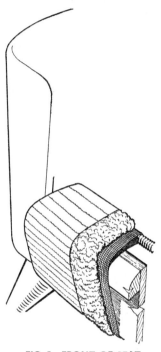

FIG. 4. UPHOLSTERY OF ARM.

Alternative methods of fixing seat springs
are shown.

FIG. 5. FRONT OF SEAT.

Note hessian taken round first spring
and back.

of the front cover to fit the front. Also cut two small borders or side facings to fit the sides of the front cover. Remove from the frame and join up with a piping inserted. The inside backs, inside and outside wings are straightforward cuts, no fitting for piping being required.

Make certain there is sufficient cover for the cushions and borders but do not cut the cushions until the suite is covered as a template is needed to obtain a well-fitting cushion.

Covering. Start the covering proper with the seats. The platform lining attached to the front edge covering is laid on the seat; pass the loose extending piece of lining under No. 1 tension spring and tack it down on the front edge rail. Tack a piece of hessian over the lining and pass it back under the first spring and over, back to the front edge again, continuing down to the lower front rail. Place several layers of linter's felt on the hessian and pull the front cover over it, fixing it with temporary tacks. Stretch the lining over the springs to the back tacking rail and the side rails. Tack this down all round but do not pull it taut sideways, and leave sufficient play to allow for the expansion of the springs in use; clean the front portion of rucks and finally tack off.

Although the settee seat springs are fixed from back to front the seat covering can be carried out in a similar manner, but with this difference—there is no spring from side to side to pull the lining and hessian under. Therefore stretch a folded web from side rail to side rail at the same distance as the spring is on the easy frame and use it as a spring for holding the cover in place.

Arm covering. Cover the arms next, using a layer of 1 in. rubberized hair or a sheet of foamed latex 1 in. thick. Whichever is being used, cut to shape and fix in place, using a spot of *Bostik* or similar adhesive here and there to hold it in position. The hair can be held with tacks along the edges and should be graduated off to the lower tacking rails. A layer of linter's felt is required over hair, but it is not necessary over latex sheeting. Lay the fitted cover over gently, and gradually draw it over into position, holding it in place with a few fixing tacks. Clean out and tack off on the lower tacking rails but leave free on the outsides. Complete both arms to this stage before starting on the back.

Whether rubberized hair, hair pads, or fibre pads are used, two good layers of linter's felt will be needed to obtain really good backs. Before placing the linter's felt on the back, tuck the lower end of the inside back cover through the tacking rails and fix on the back tacking rail with about three temporary tacks. Lay the remainder of the cover back on the seat. Place the linter's felt in position, and draw the back over to the top rail fixing there and down the sides on the uprights: pull taut and clean all round, but not so tightly as to spoil the shape, and tack off. Tie in three buttons equally spaced across the back of each easy in a line about level with the top of the arm (five are used across the settee back). Use a mattress needle and twine, pulling down tight with a slip knot.

The wings can be all linter's felt, a good thick double layer. Fix the cover on the back upright and pull over to the front, then clean out upwards and downwards, using temporary tacks until all rucks are cleaned out. Tack down but do not pull down too hard as it spoils the comfort of a soft wing.

Outside. Having completed the covering of the front of the chair or settee, the outsides and finishing off can be proceed with. Make up some lengths of piping and tack it round the front edges of the wings and the top of the back. Use fine tacks, either $\frac{3}{8}$ in or $\frac{1}{2}$ in.,

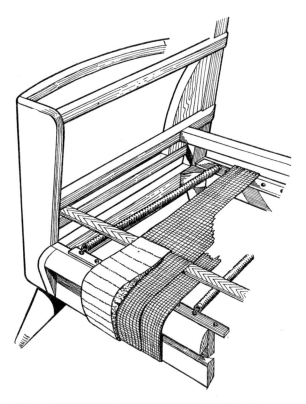

FIG. 6. HOW SETTEE SEAT SPRINGING IS ARRANGED.

for tacking off the covers. Fix the outside wings along the front edges close to the piping, tack off at the lower edge on the arm rail and on the back uprights, the piping on the top of the outside arm being pulled across the wing and tacked on the rear side of the back upright. Similarly, the outside arm is also tacked off all round, pulling the fabric taut and clean.

Complete the tacking off of the outside wings and arms before proceeding with the outside backs, which are back-tacked along the top of the top back rail close to the piping and pulled to the lower rail, tacking off on the underside. The side edges are turned in and can be gimp-pinned down or preferably slip-stiched. Use a small half circular needle and strong carpet thread making tight stitches not too close together. Finish the outside wings by slip-stitching and the lower part of the arms where they finish below the seat level. A calico or light hessian bottom completes the upholstery.

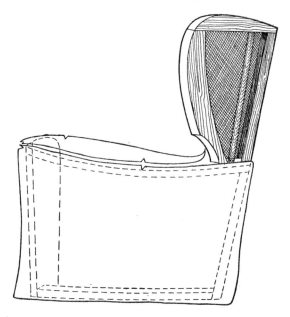

FIG. 7. CUTTING AND FITTING INSIDE AND OUTSIDE ARMS.

The legs could be finished with black polish, preferably a dull or satin black. Flat castors of the "quad" type could be fitted, or the brass ferrules with an adjustable toe which give an elegant finishing touch.

Cushions. Take a template of the seats with stiff paper, and lay it on the cover allotted for the cushions: cut round the template, leaving a $\frac{3}{8}$ in. or $\frac{1}{2}$ in. sewing allowance all round. Foamed latex cushions are suggested as being the most suitable and you should cut the borders fairly tightly so that a smart cushion is obtained. If there is enough cover to cut the piping on the cross or bias it will be worth while doing so as it gives a much better finish to the cushions.

(*Fabric cutting list appears on page 145*)

CHAPTER XX

SPRING UNIT OR PATENT-SPRUNG UPHOLSTERY

SEVERAL methods of upholstery can be applied when assembling an easy chair or settee on a foundation of pre-formed spring units. The first or scrim stuffing is reduced to a minimum and often dispensed with altogether. This is particularly so when using hair or fibre pads.

In this case it is proposed to use loose stuffing in conjunction with a double-sprung wire-mesh spring unit for the seat, calico pocketed

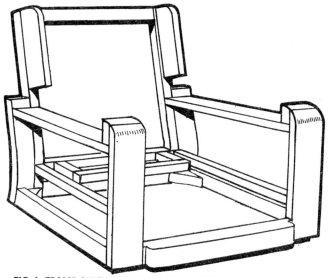

FIG. I. FRAME SUITABLE FOR PATENT-SPRUNG UPHOLSTERY.

or hessian wall, and pocketed spring units for the arms. These units are made up of two rows of $4\frac{1}{2}$-in. by 15-gauge springs, each spring being approximately 3 in. in diameter. Another hessian-covered unit is required for the back, made up with 6-in. by 15-gauge springs, the top and bottom coils having diameters of about $4\frac{1}{2}$ in. This back unit requires a flange of hessian round its outside edges, top and bottom, for tacking to the frame.

First stuffing: Arms and back. Fig. 1 shows a frame suit-able for unit springing. Start with a piece of web across the centre of each arm, tacking to the front of the tacking rail and straining up to the top arm rail.   Fix the hessian in a similar manner, bottom rail to the top one, then from the back to the front upright.   The spring units for the arms are next stapled to the top arm rails.   These can be first stuffed straightway with a light layer of hair or fibre, picked on, under loops of twine and covered with scrim.   Run a series of mattress stitches along the top and a row each side so that the stuffing is pulled up to the top coils of the springs.

The back has two webs spaced an equal distance from the centre, tacked to the front of the back tacking rail, and strained to the front of the top back rail.   The spring unit for the back is placed in position and held there temporarily with a few tacks partly driven home.   Pull the lower bottom flange of the unit round the back tacking rail and tack it to the back of this rail.   Tack the lower top flange to the top edge of the top back rail, keeping the tacks as near the front edge as possible.   The lower side flanges are tacked to the front edge of the back upright, but only from the top to the top arm rail.

Double over all the hessian, particularly the side flanges when tacking.   In fact, it is as well to tack the latter down turned over, then turn them over again and tack down so that the tacks do not cut through the hessian.   The top flanges are dealt with next, the lower one being tacked to the blocked-out back rail.   Tack the top flange to the top of the back rail, turning under the hessian for neatness.   Deal with the side flanges in a similar manner, tacking them to the facing blocks.   Leave the bottom portion of these side flanges until the covering is finished.   All the bottom flanges should be tacked off as tightly as possible, but do not pull the top ones too taut—just sufficient to keep the coils of the springs even.

Pencil a line round the top portion of the back about 5 in. in from the facings, also down from the edge of the top springs.   Cut a strip of scrim about 9 in. in width and sew it along the pencil marks with running stitches about 1 in. in length, using a half-circular needle and fine mattress twine.   After completing the stitching, lay the scrim back and pick a small amount of stuffing under it, then pull the scrim over and fix it all round temporarily.   Even out the stuffing where necessary, not too heavy along the top, but fairly tightly packed round the facings.   Tack the top to the outer edge of the back rail and the sides to the outer edge of the facings.   These sides are stitched into an edge or roll with a sink stitch and a top stitch.   A single stitch along the top edge should be small so that the roll does not project over too much.   Fig. 2 shows the back and arms of the chair with hessian-covered units, lightly stuffed.

The seat. The seat is the next item. This can be first stuffed before finally fixing it in position. Cut a piece of hessian long enough to cover from the back seat rail over the unit to the bottom front rail and about 3 in. wider than the unit. Place the hessian over the seat, keeping it in position with a few skewers spaced two or three to each side. Using a spring needle, make a series of half-hitches all round the wired edge on the top of the unit, keeping the hessian taut. Do the same across the middle wire edge at the front. After

FIG. 2. HOW ARMS AND BACK ARE SPRUNG.
The spring units are covered with hessian and lightly first stuffed.

this the usual series of loops for stringing in the stuffing is made round the top, about 2 in. from the edges as in Fig. 3.

Pick the stuffing under these loops and fill in the centre lightly. Unit-sprung work does not require such a heavy stuffing as hand-sprung work, except on rolls and edges. The scrim is laid over, held in place temporarily with skewers round the edges, and run through. Make certain that no running-through twine catches a rung of the springs. Work all round the seat, fixing the scrim with skewers and levelling out the stuffing where necessary. The scrim can be stitched across the front edge with a fine twine and a half-circular needle. The sides and back edges of the scrim are attached to the spring hessian at the same time as the sink or blind stitch is made.   The needle is inserted under the wire and returned to under the wire, thus pulling the stuffing over the wire to a certain extent. Along the front the usual method is adopted with both the sink and top stitches.   No top stitch is required round the back and sides, but the front edge needs one to mould it to a firm, even roll.

The seat can also be top stuffed and covered with calico in this position.   Run three lines of twine across the seat for stringing in the stuffing.   At the present time good quality clean hair is still the best of top stuffings and for the most other stuffings where the price will allow.   Pick it under the twines evenly, but at the same time knead

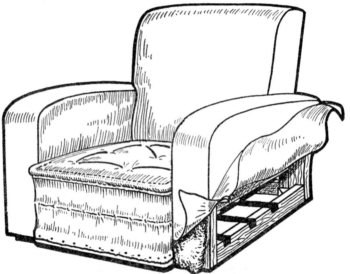

FIG. 3. COVERING OF ARMS AND BACK.
This also shows the first or scrim stuffing of the seat.

or merge it together to form an even layer of stuffing of a concave shape.   Cover this with a light-grade calico and secure temporarily with skewers.   Afterwards sew with a half-circular needle just under the edge, stitching all round the back, sides, and front.

The completed unit is ready for fixing in position, but first fix the three loose laths to the frame with 1-in. clouts or wall nails. Wind a piece of soft material, hessian or scrim, round each lath before fixing, so ensuring that no noise is caused by the base of the unit rubbing against the laths already fixed.

Top stuffing and covering.   The completion of the top stuffing and the covering can now be carried out.   These operations differ little from the methods adopted with the hand-sprung work. The various sections of the chair are measured and the cover is cut to the required sizes. It is flyed and sewn in the usual way. Sometimes it is more convenient to top stuff and cover the arms and back before fixing the seat in position. If the cover sizes are known and the cover is sewn ready for fixing in position before starting on the frame, it is generally easier and quicker to complete the first and second stuffing of the arms, likewise the back and finally the seat.

Pick the stuffing on under the usual loops of twine. Keep the top stuffing "light"—a fair quantity on the seat but a much lighter amount on the arms and back. The wire mesh over the springs does away with the "bony" feel so often noticed on hand-sprung work that is too lightly stuffed. Where pocket springing is used there is little fear of its being bony if a light layer of stuffing is used. Hair or fibre covered with linter's felt or wadding are the usual fillings for spring-unit work. Flocks or ruggings are not satisfactory over wire-mesh-covered units.

The use of hair or fibre pads. A similar job can be carried out using hair or fibre pads and linter's felt only. No first stuffing, as it is generally understood. The arms are webbed as usual, then a hessian pad is tacked on the bottom rail and pulled up and over the springs. A few tacks are placed along both sides of the top arm rail to hold the hessian in place. If it is intended to stuff the outside arm the pad is left long enough to reach the side seat rail. Do not tack off on this rail yet, but leave until the seat and inside arms are finished. The back springing is also covered with a pad tacked on the bottom tacking rail, top back rail, and round the facings. As a rule the only other stuffing required on the back and arms is a good layer of linter's felt.

A slightly different method is used on the seat. The pad is drawn over and caught with a few ties round the edge wire of the spring unit. Before covering this with linter's felt a substantial layer of loose stuffing is picked on the pad. The covering is all carried out as previously described, excepting it does not need to be pulled down quite so taut as over loose stuffing. It is easier to cover a chair or settee assembled with hair or fibre interwoven on hessian. There is little chance of the stuffing becoming displaced as is the case with loose stuffing unless it is carefully dealt with. Less fixing with temporary tacks is required, as the stuffing is already in place and does not need much pulling down. The surface under the pads must be even, otherwise a lot of loose stuffing will be needed, thus defeating the object of a quick and easy method. Fig. 3 shows the covering.

CHAPTER XXI

ALTERNATIVE BUILD-UPS AND CUSHION INTERIORS

APART from the previously described methods of building up upholstery there are several alternatives. Most of these are governed by the construction of the seat units. One of the most popular is the combination of short tension springs, vertical cone springs, and hessian-covered pocketed springs (see Fig. 1). The

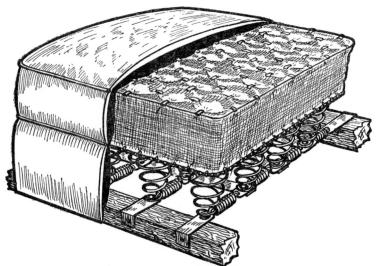

FIG. I. COMBINATION OF POCKET SPRINGS, CONE SPRINGS, AND TENSION SPRINGS.

stuffings most frequently used with these units are hair or fibre pads with a final layer of linter's felt. In most cases the pad is tacked at the back seat rail and brought over to the front seat rail, forming a quick and easy method of stuffing which gives a good seat. A little extra loose stuffing is often required on a seat of this type before the linter's felt is placed into position. Hair or fibre needlepointed on hessian forms a ready-made stuffing and is becoming almost standard practice.

Tension spring. Pocketed springing in conjunction with tension

or cable springs is another combination frequently used (Fig. 2).
When this method is adopted the frames must be built up with the
side rails set at a correct height to take the tension or cable springs.
The number of springs varies according to the size and often the
quality of the job.   Seven on a fireside chair is usual and eight or nine
on the larger easies.   It is essential that the seat rails taking the strain
of the springs should be strong and properly fitted.

The important difference between an ordinary coil spring and one

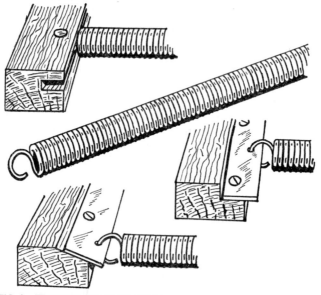

FIG. 2.   TENSION OR CABLE SPRINGS AND THEIR ATTACHMENT.
The method of attachment must be ascertained before frame is made as groove
rebate or chamfer may be required.

of the tension type is that the former takes the weight by compres-
sion whereas the latter does so by expansion.   Some firms use a pair
of metal plates drilled with the required number of holes for fixing
the springs to the frame as in Fig. 2.   The plates are screwed to the
side seat rails, making a neat, sturdy job, especially for fireside chairs
having a loose cushion seat.   Another method is to groove the rails and
fix the springs inside the groove by driving a nail through from the
top of the rails (see Fig. 2).   Where the actual fixing is not seen it is
often done with clouts, small wall nails, or staples.

When pocket springs are used over tension springs to form a tight
covered seat, that is, without a loose cushion, a piece of hessian is

tacked over the tension springs first. This must not be stretched tightly from side to side, but left slack to allow for the deflection of the springs. This hessian is also required when using rubberized hair or fibre. A method often applied when using loose stuffing over tension springing is to make a scrim or hessian bag, filling it with stuffing, then making a few ties with twine to keep the stuffing in place. This is tacked into position, allowing ample play or slack. Most surfaces need a layer of wadding or linter's felt before the covering is fixed.

When a loose cushion is required a platform over the springs is made from a lining or other suitable material to tone with the covering material. One method is to enclose each spring in a pocket sewn on the lining. Another method is to make two pockets only, one at the front and one at the back of the platform lining. Insert the rear spring into its pocket and fix it in position. Bring the platform over the other springs already fixed, and insert the front but one spring into the front pocket. To cover the front spring and front rail, tack one edge of the cover to the top of the front rail. Pass the other end under and then over the first spring. Before returning it to the front rail, lay a piece of wadding or linter's felt along the space between the spring and the front edge of the rail. Bring the cover over the whole and tack it to the underside of the front rail. These are the methods frequently used on fireside easy chairs.

Spring interior loose cushion. The loose cushion with a spring interior is built up in the same manner whether for use with a coil or cable spring base. There are several types of spring units for cushion work, with either open mesh, calico, or hessian pocketed springs approximately 3 in. in diameter and varying between 3 and 4 in. in height. Deeper springs units are also obtainable for special jobs. The cushion case is cut to a template or to measurements taken on the chair or settee, due allowances being made for sewing. A double thickness of linter's felt is wrapped round the spring interior and the whole is inserted into the case.

Most firms have a cushion-filling machine, but occasionally a cushion has to be filled by hand. When this is necessary about a third of the bottom of the case must be left unsewn. This is slip-stitched to the borders after the mass of linter's and springing has been inserted. Rubber cushioning and rubberized hair also form good interiors for cushions. Neither of these should give much trouble, as they are either moulded or cut to shape.

Feather cushion. Feather cushions were extensively used before the advent of spring interiors. Properly filled with good-quality feathers they give years of comfortable service. An inside case of down-proof calico is required for feather or down cushions. The down-proof case would be cut about 1 in. larger all round than the outer case. It should be divided into compartments, thus helping to keep the feathers where they are most required. For example, a cushion 20 in. wide by 24 in. deep would have three compartments, the front and middle ones being well filled but the back one not quite so full.

Be generous when cutting the divisions, which can be of either down-proof or ordinary calico. Allow about 2 in. more in depth than the outside border, as there is a tendency to drag down which will show too distinctly on the outer case.

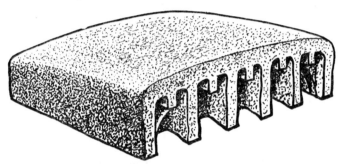

FIG. 3. SECTION THROUGH MOULDED LATEX CUSHIONING.
Although initial cost may be greater than other materials, the time saved in their use saves much expense.

Latex rubber, etc. Apart from cushion work, moulded latex rubber and rubberized hair cushioning are likely to be important rivals to the old-style stuffings. There is undoubtedly room in the upholstery fillings list for both these materials, and for some work they are to be preferred. Both can be used over springs and both are practically insect proof. Rubberized hair is lighter than foamed latex rubber, and requires a layer of linter's felt or wadding over it before final covering. Fig. 3 shows a section through a moulded latex cushion.

Little upholstery skill is required in the use of these materials, as they are usually cut to the required shape and it only remains to fix them into position. The covering of rubber cushioning offers no great difficulties. Piped finishes wherever possible make for clean lines. On wide surfaces fluting makes an attractive finish and helps to avoid showing any bagginess as the cover stretches in use.

Resilient webbing. Another important addition to the wide range of upholstery components is the rubber web. It is built up of rubber and fabric bonded together in a similar manner to a motor tyre. The two layers of fabric are cut at opposing angles and sandwiched with rubber, forming a strong and resilient type of webbing.

Made in five widths, $2\frac{1}{4}$ in., 2 in., $1\frac{1}{2}$ in., $1\frac{3}{8}$ in., and $\frac{3}{4}$ in., it can be used successfully on many different types of job. The wider widths are suitable for seats and the narrow widths for arms and backs.

There are several ways of fixing it to upholstery frames. The simplest on wooden frames is with $\frac{5}{8}$-in. improved tacks or clout nails, three or four on the wider widths, and two on the narrow ones. Drive the tacks well home and cut off the webs approximately $\frac{1}{4}$ in. beyond the tacks. It must be stretched or tensioned into place and this tension can be varied to form the type of seating required.

The degree of firmness or softness required in a seat or back is governed by the amount of strain or tension placed on the webbing when fixing into position. A lightly strained webbed seat will be much softer than the tightly stretched one. At the same time it is obvious that over wide spaces the webs must be more tightly stretched, such as on a settee seat or across a divan.

The traditional method of using webbing in upholstery has been to interlace side-to-side webs with back to front webs. This can be forgotten when using rubber webbing; it needs treating more as a spring than a web. Therefore on short spans the web can be used one way only, either back to front or side to side, much as a tension spring would be used. On wide spans, however, it is advisable to interlace as well as to increase the tension, though the number of webs required will be less than on an ordinary webbed seat.

Although tacking on the web is the simplest method of fixing there are other effective ways. It can be obtained pre-cut to the size required with a steel clip attached to each end. These ends are inserted in a groove cut at an angle of approximately 15 degrees. Likewise a wire clip is made for attachment to metal frames and tubular frames.

As with the foams there are several firms making rubber webbing and their products are of a good standard.

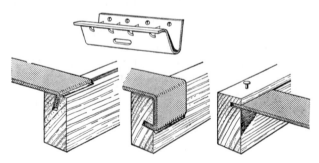

FIG. 4. METHODS OF ATTACHING PIRELLI RUBBER WEBS.

CHAPTER XXII

BOX OTTOMAN

THE idea of the box ottoman is old, but there are many modern variations of the notion of making a box with an upholstered lid. The box forms a dustproof storage for clothes and linen, whilst the top or lid makes a comfortable seat. It can also be used as an emergency bed for a child. A useful all-round size is 4 ft. 3 in. long over-all by 1 ft. 10 in. wide, with an inside depth of almost 9 in.

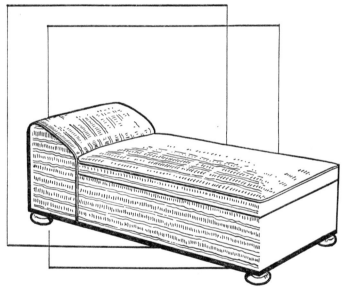

FIG. I.   USEFUL ITEM WITH GOOD STORAGE SPACE.
Over-all size is 4 ft. 3 in. long, 1 ft. 10 in. wide and 1 ft. 7 in. high over the head.
A piece of this type is useful both for storage space and as an occasional seat.

Making the box. Make up the box to the required size, dovetailing the ends to the sides or, as usually happens in commercial jobs, gluing and nailing them. The head-rest is cut to shape and dowelled to the box. Stiffen each corner with a triangular-sectioned fillet glued and screwed in position. The bottom boards are temporarily nailed on the bottom edges of the framing. For the framing use ⅞-in. planed softwood; the bottom can be one piece of ⅜-in. ply if available, or ⅝-in. by 6-in. deal laid widthways.

The lid is made to fit, using $\frac{7}{8}$-in. by $3\frac{1}{2}$-in. material for the frame and $\frac{7}{8}$-in. by 3-in. for the five spring rails. These are dovetailed and screwed to the bottom edges of the lid framing. Four feet cut to shape and bored for the screws complete the woodwork. See Fig. 2 for details.

Springs. Three 5-in. by 11-gauge springs are stapled to each rail, with a piece of hessian or soft material tacked on the rails first to form an anti-knock. A box ottoman does not have heavy wear as a rule, but it is advisable to lace the springs in position with a laid cord. Cover them with a fairly stout hessian, tacking it on temporarily before finally tacking down with $\frac{1}{2}$-in. improved tacks. Keep the

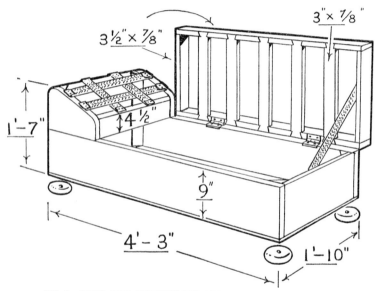

FIG. 2. SIZES AND WOODWORK DETAILS OF BOX AND LID.

tacks close to the outside edge of the framing and leave about $2\frac{1}{2}$ in. of hessian overhanging. Sew the springs to the hessian with the usual three ties.

Top stuffing. Lay a small quantity of fibre on the overhanging piece of hessian and roll it over to form an even roll or edge about the size of the thumb. This is continued all round the edge and is tacked down with $\frac{5}{8}$-in. tacks. A series of loops of twine are made all round the lid just inside this roll. A top stuffing of hair, flock, or fibre is picked under these loops, also over the central portion of the seat. Cover the whole with a light hessian or calico. This is temporarily fixed in position and finally tacked off on the outside of the framing.

The head is the next item. Tack on and strain two webs each way, using $\frac{5}{8}$-in. improved tacks. A piece of hessian is tacked over the webs, being strained on as tightly as possible. Make the usual loops of twine round the edge and pick a thin layer of stuffing under them. Cover with hessian or calico similarly to the seat.

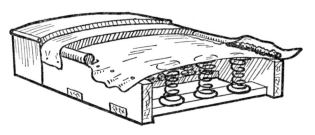

FIG. 3. SECTIONAL VIEW THROUGH LID.
This shows springs, hessian, thumb rolls, top stuffing, calico, linter's felt ,and cover with piped edge.

FIG. 4. DETAILS OF LINING, BOX SHOWN UPSIDE-DOWN.

Lining the box. Lining, or covering the inside of the box must now be dealt with. A strong cotton material is most suitable if obtainable. Remove the bottom boards before starting the lining, as it is tacked on the bottom edge of the box framing. Start by cutting four strips to cover the corner fillets. Tack these on the bottom and pull as tight as possible to the top edges.

Only three or four tacks will be required on the sides of these corner pieces, provided they are strained on tightly. Continue with the sides and ends in a similar manner, tacking on the bottom edge and straining to the top. At the point where the fillet linings are met do not tack, but fold under and crease well. Then strain as tightly as possible top and bottom and the lining will remain in place without tacking. The bottom piece of lining is laid over the open space of the bottom and tacked on all round the box framing.

The outside cover. The lining completed, the outer cover is the next operation, but first replace and fix the bottom boards. The outer cover is started on the inside of the box about $\frac{1}{2}$ in. down. Cut some $\frac{1}{2}$-in. strips of cardboard and back-tack through these strips. Draw the cover over the top edge and tack off on the bottom. Repeat this procedure with both sides and one end.

The head is covered separately as it is cut to shape and piped. Cut the top panel to size and the two side panels or facings, allowing $\frac{1}{2}$ in. all round for sewing. Piping is sewn along the top and two sides of both facings and the top panel is joined to them.

Lay a piece of wadding or linter's felt over the head and pull the cover over. Tack it off at the back and front, also through the piping seams at the sides. This is done by throwing the two facings back over the head so that it is possible to tack through the seams. The facings are turned back and fixed in place. Tack off on the bottom and along the outside edges. The other edges must be slip-stitched to the main side cover. Finish the outside end by back-tacking along the top edge and slip-stitching the sides to the piping on the facings. Turn the ottoman over and cover the bottom with hessian neatly turned in and tacked. Fix four short contemporary style turned legs near each corner. These should be polished to harmonise with the room furniture and fitted with Armstrong "Quads," or similar type of flat movable castor. This completes the box covering and the lid can be proceeded with next.

Cover. The cover can be made up with a piping round the top edge or pulled over in one piece and the corners folded in. Whichever way is decided upon a layer of wadding is the first requirement. Pull the cover over and fix in place all round, finally tacking off on the underside of the lid. This completed, the inside of the lid is lined with the same lining as the box interior. Tack a piece of light hessian over the spring rails and place a thin layer of wadding or linter's felt on the hessian. The lining can then be tacked on using $\frac{1}{2}$-in. gimp pins all round, or it may be back-tacked along the front edge and gimp-pinned on the remaining edges.

A small tab of the covering material can be made, or a fancy handle fitted for lifting the lid if desired. The final operations are fitting the hinges and a staying tape or light chain to prevent the lid overbalancing when in the open position.

CHAPTER XXIII

DIVAN BED

THE divan bed has largely taken the place of the separate head and foot and metal sides. Used in conjunction with a spring interior mattress it is certainly very comfortable.

Frame. Making the frame is the first job. The width sizes vary from 2 ft. 6 in. to 4 ft. 6 in., but the usual length is 6 ft. 2 in. Planed $\frac{7}{8}$-in. deal, beech, or ramin is suggested for the main rails, and oak, birch, or beech for the feet or stumps. The headboard can be

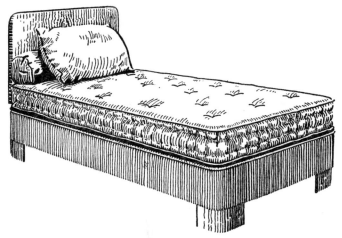

FIG. I. A POPULAR FORM OF BED.

This can be made in all sizes from 2 ft. 6 in. up to 4 ft. 6 in. The length remains constant at 6 ft. 2 in.

shaped and made up of $\frac{3}{4}$-in. blockboard, or one of the firmer chipboards and upholstered. As the divan base is intended to support a spring interior mattress a suitable height is about 12 in. The headboard should be 34 in. from the floor to the top when in position. Cut the headboard to shape and fit two supports to the back after covering. The supports should be 24 in. by 2 in. by $\frac{7}{8}$ in.

The frame in the design has rounded feet and corners. Each of these is shaped out of one piece 10 in. by 8 in. by 3 in. placed diagonally across the corners. Round each stump and rebate the two sides

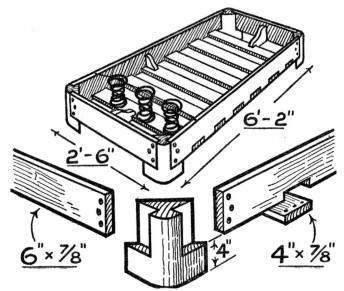

FIG. 2. DETAILS OF THE FRAME.

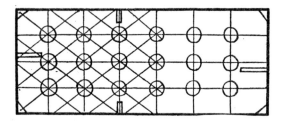

FIG. 3. ALTERNATIVE METHODS OF LACING SPRINGS.

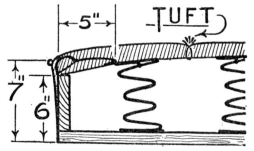

FIG. 4. SECTION SHOWING SPRINGS AND STUFFING.

to receive the end and side rails as shown in Fig. 2. The over-all sizes of the frame given here are 6 ft. 2 in. by 2 ft. 6 in., and the rail sizes ⅞ in. by 6 in.

Six cross rails for the springs are needed, these being ⅞ in. by 4 in. Cut off the two side rails first and mark out to receive the springing rails. Space these 7 in. apart excepting the two end ones which are 7½ in. from the outside edge of the frame (Fig. 2). Glue and screw the end and side rails to the legs, also the spring rails to the side rails. Make sure the frame is perfectly square when glued up, then fit two shaped blocks at the sides and one at each end as shown.

Springing. First tack a 4-in. wide strip of hessian across each rail to prevent the springs from making a noise. Three 7-in. by 9- or 10-gauge springs to each rail, making eighteen in all, are required. Secure these to the framing by staples, three to each spring. The two side rows of springs are placed about 4 in. from the inside of the frame. These are laced or lashed in position with laid cord or other strong, non-stretching cord. Start lacing from side to side, first knocking a staple partly home opposite the centre of each row of springs. Thread an end of cord through these staples along one side, making each fast with a tie, then driving the staples home. Staples hold better than tacks for this job and do not split the deal so much.

Bring the cord to the top rung of the first spring and either knot or make a hitch round the wire. Proceed across each row of springs in this way, keeping the centre springs perfectly upright. The side springs all round should incline slightly towards the outside edge of the frame. After lacing crosswise proceed with lengthwise lacing, using the same method. Where the cords pass over each other take a single turn round the one already fixed. On a first-class job the springs would also be diagonally laced. This requires careful judgment to ensure the correct positioning of the springs, as all the lacing cords must be kept to an equal tension (Fig. 3).

Hessian. When this has been completed proceed to hessian, using a stout quality, preferably the kind called tarpaulin. Fix it all round with temporary tacks first, then tack off the raw edge with ¾-in. improved tacks. Leave about ⅞ in. of spare hessian when trimming off, turning this over afterwards and tacking down. If the springs are diagonally laced it is not necessary to sew them to the hessian, otherwise sew in with three ties each, using a stout twine and spring needle. A small roll or edge all round is the next item, and this can either be of the tacked-on variety or a single-stitched type. To form the latter stitch a piece of scrim or cheap hessian on to the spring hessian. Turn under the raw edge and keep it parallel about

5 in. from the edge of the frame. Stitch down with a half-circular needle and thin twine, making fairly long running stitches.

Stuffing. Pick sufficient fibre under the scrim to bring the edge level with top of the centre springs. Do this all round, fixing with temporary tacks until a firm, even edge is obtained, then tacking down. Tack with ½-in. improved tacks along a line about 1 in. down on the outside of the frame. Regulate the stuffing well forward with a regulator or stout needle and make a single stitch all round. Start from the left-hand end, pushing the needle through close to the frame, taking up about 1½ in. of scrim on top before returning and making a slip-knot. Pull tight and carry the needle along 3 in. before inserting again. Return the needle about 1½ in. behind its point of entry and this time make a single twist around the needle as it comes through. Carry on round the frame in this manner, pulling the twine tight to form an even edge.

Cover. When this operation has been completed it is advisable

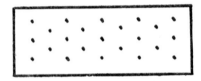

FIG. 5. POSITION OF TUFTS.

to cut and fit the cover. Mattress ticking is the usual covering but latterly other materials have been used with various results. Ticking is approximately 58 in. wide, and 3 yards will be required. Cut the top piece 6 ft. 4 in. by 2 ft. 8 in., thus allowing for the top stuffing and for stitching. Lay this piece on the job and shape the corners, not forgetting the allowances.

Next cut the border pieces about 9 in. deep, three pieces being required. One width halved for each end and one width with a piece joined to each end for the side borders. Cut from the waste of the top for these joining portions. The borders are joined to the centre piece with a piped edge between. Make this up with odd pieces of tick cut on the cross about 1¼ in. wide. The top and sides are now machined together forming a piped, boxed border all round.

Top stuffing. A thin top stuffing all over is the next item. Hair or fibre covered with a layer of linter's felt or a felted flock are all suitable. Run a few loops of twine round the edges about 2 in. in, and pick a thin, even amount of stuffing under these. Lightly fill in the centre with an even layer of stuffing so that the tops of the springs can almost be felt, and cover with linter's felt, placing the cover over all, and easing down gently until the borders are in position. Temporarily tack all round then pull down further and tack again until the piped edge is level with the stitched edge.

The top is next marked out for tufting. Wool tufts give the nicest finish but cotton tufts or upholstery buttons can be used. Push a straight mattress needle through the tick to the spring hessian, catching about $\frac{3}{4}$ in. of the latter before returning. Tie a slip-knot on top and cut the twine, leaving about 6 in. beyond the knot. Proceed to all the tufting points similarly before pushing the tufts under the slip-knots. Pull the knots tight and secure by knotting the twine before cutting off. Fig. 5 shows the position of the tufts.

The divan can now be turned on edge and the cover tacked down on the underside with $\frac{1}{2}$-in. fine tacks. Finish off with a hessian bottom, turning under the raw edges and tacking off evenly.

The headboard. Having completed the base carry on with the headboard. This can be covered with a soft material if desired or one of the many designs of P.V.C. coated fabrics. There are numerous bright and gay, washable P.V.C. fabrics available. Bore five $\frac{1}{4}$ in. holes equally spaced approximately 8 in. from the top of the headboard. The buttoning needle and twine are pulled through the holes. Two layers of linter's felt or an inch thickness of polyether foam can be laid on the board. The cover chosen can be placed over the felt or foam and gradually pulled into position and fixed with temporary tacks. Pull taut and clean out any creases before tacking down on the back of the board. The buttons are fixed in place by passing a mattress needle and twine through the buttons then through the holes already made in the headboard, thus making a double twine through to the back where it is twisted round a tack and the tack driven home. The twine must be kept tight so the button is sunk as much as possible. The outside back should be covered either with the same material or a piece of lining tacked in place with gimp pins.

Fix the two supports or uprights in position by screwing them into place on the back of the board approximately 6 in. inwards from the edges. Two headboard brackets should be screwed on to the divan base to engage the uprights.

CHAPTER XXIV

SPRING INTERIOR MATTRESS AND SPRING BASE

THIS is intended for use in conjunction with the usual bed head and foot, the base resting upon the metal sides. It could be used as a divan bed, however, by fitting corner legs in the angles. The softwood frame is made like a shallow box-spring mattress. Standard length is 6 ft. 2 in., whilst the width is according to the size of the bed, 3 ft., 3 ft. 6 in., 4 ft., or 4 ft. 6 in. The sides and ends require 1-in. by 5-in. planed softwood, and the slats for the springs at least 1-in. by 3½-in., preferably 1-in. by 4-in. material.

Making the frame. The two side members are cut to size, marked out, and cut for the bottom slats. Six slats are usual on the 3-ft. size and seven for the 4-ft. 6-in. base. The sides are joined to the ends with a box dovetail or, more frequently, butted, glued, and nailed.

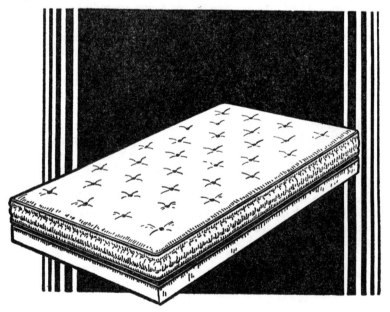

FIG. I. AN EXTREMELY COMFORTABLE FORM OF MATTRESS.
Made to the standard size of 6 ft. 2 in. long by a width of 3 ft., 3 ft. 6 in., 4 ft., or 4 ft. 6 in.

Ascertain whether the frame is square and nail a spline across diagonally to keep it in position whilst two or three slats are fixed. These are glued and screwed in place. A block fixed in each corner and a bracket in the centre of each end and side rail will help to make a rigid frame. Fig. 2 shows the completed frame.

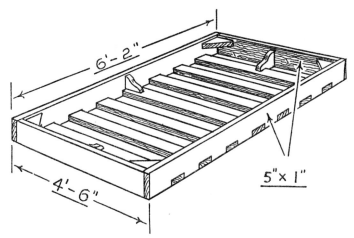

FIG. 2. FRAME CONSTRUCTION SHOWING SPRING RAILS.

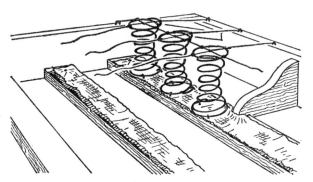

FIG. 3. HOW THE SPRINGS ARE LACED TOGETHER.
Note the hessian or soft material beneath the springs to act as an anti-knock device.

The Spring Base. A fairly flat, shallow-sprung even surface is the ultimate requirement of a base. By using 5-in. by 10-gauge springs this should be obtained. Cover the top of each slat with a piece of hessian, fixing it with two tacks at each end. This is to prevent the springs making a noise if the bottom rungs hit the wood. Each

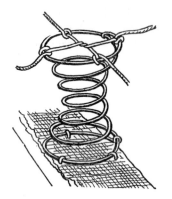

FIG. 4. TIES USED FOR LACING SPRINGS.

A stronger alternative is to knot each tie, but is more difficult to alter if the springs are not quite in position when the cord is pulled tight and fastened. By using the method shown the springs can be moved a trifle either way without undoing all the knots.

FIG. 5. HOW TUFTS ARE TIED.

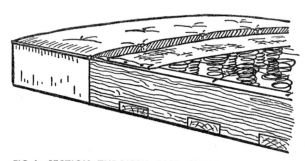

FIG. 6. SECTION THROUGH BASE, SHOWING SPRINGS, HESSIAN, STUFFING, TUFTS, AND COVER.

spring is fastened in position with three staples, the number of springs being governed by the width of the frame. A single, or 3-ft., size would need four springs to each slat, making 24 springs in all. The double, or 4-ft. 6-in., size requires six springs to each slat, that is 42 in all. When the springs are all stapled in place the top coils are laced in position with a stout laid cord or strong sisal four-ply twine. Fig. 3 shows the springs in position, whilst Fig. 4 gives the lacing.

Work from side to side first, cutting off lengths of laid cord about 15 in. longer than the width of the base. Fix by driving a staple in the top edge of the frame opposite each row of springs. The cord is passed through the staple, knotted, and the staple driven home.

Bring the cord to the first spring, make a tie on each side of the top coil, and continue across each row in this manner. Pull the cord taut when passing through the staple before driving the staple home. At the same time make sure each spring is upright excepting those nearest the framing, these can lean a little outwards. Repeat the lacing from end to end, thus holding each spring in position with four ties on each top coil. This completed, the top surface is covered with a fairly stout hessian pulled over tightly and tacked down with $\frac{5}{8}$-in. improved tacks or small $\frac{1}{2}$-in. clout nails.

The stuffing and covering. At this stage the covering material, either a ticking or similar soft material, can be cut to size and prepared for sewing. The cover can be laid over the hessian and fixed in place with a few temporary tacks. Mark along each edge with a piece of chalk and cut to within $\frac{1}{2}$ in. of this line, thus making the sewing allowance. Alternatively, the cover can be cut by measurement, always remembering the sewing allowance.

Cut the borders next to fit all round the top. They are cut the depth of the sides plus $\frac{1}{2}$ in. sewing allowance and $\frac{1}{2}$ in. or slightly more for tacking off on the bottom. Machine stitch the borders to the top, inserting a piping between the two. A contrasting colour in the piping gives a good effect and can also be used round the spring interior mattress which will be dealt with later.

A series of loops of twine are made around the hessian about $2\frac{1}{2}$ in. inwards from the edge. Pick an even thickness of stuffing under this twine all round the edge. Fill in the centre of the hessian with a similar picking of stuffing not quite so thick as at the edge.

The cover is drawn carefully over the stuffing and fixed all round with temporary tacks. It is then pulled down evenly and finally tacked off along the bottom edge of the frame.

Tufting. Mark out the top for tufting, the four corner tufts being placed about 7 in. each way from the piped edge. Tufting is a simple operation using a double-pointed mattress needle and a medium twine. The needle is inserted at the required position, pulled through clear of the spring hessian and returned about $\frac{1}{2}$ in. from the point of insertion. A slip-knot is made with the twine, as in Fig. 5, and it is pulled down to the level of the cover. The tuft, either wool or cotton, is passed under the knot, and the latter pulled down as tight as possible and secured by making a knot on the twine before cutting off.

Handles. When the tufting operation is completed turn the base over so it is bottom upwards. Four web handles are fitted for convenience of handling. Cut four pieces of web about 1 ft. 6 in. in length, fold each piece in two, and fix to the first slat from each end with about five staples. The loops of web overhang the frame by 4½–5 in. Finally, a light hessian bottom is tacked on all round the frame with ½-in. tacks.

Spring interior mattress. This consists of a spring unit sandwiched between two layers of stuffing, the whole encased in a ticking or other suitable material. There are different forms of

FIG. 7. OPEN-MESH OR NON-POCKETED TYPE UNIT

FIG. 8. THE CALICO-POCKETED SPRING UNIT.

calico-pocketed spring units, also hessian-pocketed units, and the open-wire-mesh type.

Joining together. The method of joining the calico-pocketed springs together is generally by a series of ties made with a light twine. Sometimes metal clips are used for the same purpose. The top and the bottom of this form of unit are usually covered with a light calico. Similarly the open-mesh type is covered with hessian. This can be made up like a bag and the spring unit inserted, afterwards sewing up the opening. It is usual to sew round the outer edge, top and bottom, with a series of ties, using a light mattress twine. Fig. 7 gives the open-mesh unit.

The stuffings used are varied according to price and availability. Hair or hair-covered with linter's felt is the best. Efficient cheaper grade materials are coco or coir fibre pads and linter's felt, all linter's felt, all black flock, or fibre and hessian pads covered with flock felt.

Making the case. Having collected all the required materials the first item to make is the case. If it is intended to use all hair the case must be made of good quality hair ticking or other superfine material which will contain the hair. In this way the hair will not work through the material. This is important, as nothing annoys the housewife more than to find the blankets with pieces of hair on them.

The cutting sizes for the 4 ft. 6 in. mattress are 6 ft. 5 in. by 4 ft.

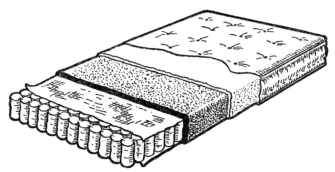

FIG. 9. THE BUILD-UP OF A POCKETED SPRING INTERIOR.

This shows the spring unit, the calico cover over the springs, a layer of fibre or hair, a layer of cotton linters, and the case or ticking cover. If black flock is used for stuffing no cotton linters is required. A layer of cotton linters is often placed over the springs before the layer of hair. Also when a good grade hair tick is available the top layer of cotton linters (or linter's felt as it is often called) is omitted and extra hair used.

8 in., which allows ½ in. all round for sewing and an extra allowance for when the tufts are tied down. This is usual on all sizes. Cut the borders 6¾ in. in depth to finish almost 6 in. when piped, which allows ½-in. turnings. It is correct to cut the piping strips on the cross, or diagonally across the material, if there is enough to spare. The border, with the piping inserted, is machined to one side of the case all round. At the other side one long edge only is stitched, thus forming a "box" of material with a lid at one side.

Spring-interior mattresses, especially the large sizes, are awkward to move unless fitted with handles. These can be made to finish about 1½ in. wide, inserted and stitched with the piping and the border at a point about 1 ft. 3 in. from each corner on the two long sides.

It is customary to fit several small eyelets for ventilation purposes.

These are stamped in with a special tool, but a small square cut in each end and seamed all round will make a good substitute.   Place a small piece of gauze or muslin behind each square hole.

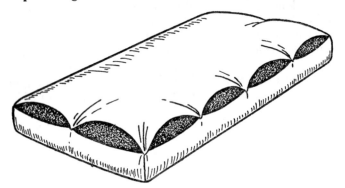

FIG. 10. HOW CASE IS TIED TEMPORARILY.
This is done before making the ties for the tufts and finally sewing the top to the borders.

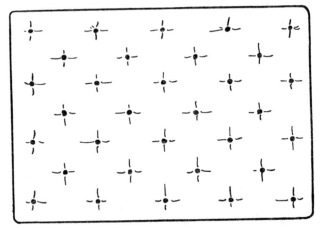

FIG. 11. LAY-OUT OF THE TUFTS DIAMOND STYLE.
5-4 length, 4-3 width is usual on 4 ft. 6 in. size.   For the 3 ft. size 5-4 and 3-2 is general.

Having completed the cutting and sewing of the case it is ready for marking out and filling.

Marking out.   Fold the case in half and mark out diamond style, starting 7 in. from the outer edge.   Five-four in the length, and four-three in the width are often used for the 4 ft. 6 in. size (see Fig. 11); five-four lengthwise and three-two in the width for the 3 ft. size.

The marking out is done on one side of the folded case, which is then pierced through with a stout needle, thus marking the other half and side at the same time.

Filling the case. Spread the case out on an even surface such as some boards laid on a pair of trestles. Fix the four corners at their fullest extent with four temporary tacks. If hair and felt are being used in a good tick place a layer of hair on the tick, then a layer of felt. When a cheaper tick is used put a layer of felt on the tick first, hair next, then a further layer of felt. The spring is placed on the top of these layers, which are repeated on the top of the springing, and the cover brought over.

Before pulling the top cover over fill in round the sides and ends evenly with stuffing. Pull the top cover over and fasten at each corner with a tie. Use a half-circular or mattress needle and twine. Continue these ties at short intervals, starting at the centre of the long side and passing to the centres of the short sides (Fig. 10). These ties are temporary and serve to fix the top cover in place whilst it is sewn to the border with a stout thread. Before this operation is started it is advisable to make the tufting ties.

During recent years loose stuffing methods have given way to ready-made pads and preformed borders in spring interior mattress production. These allow for a quicker and easier way of making a mattress and are very necessary for mass production. It does not necessarily mean a better product; loose hair can be much more resilient than hair needled to hessian. Against this, the machine-quilted, top mattress will probably oust the older tufting method completely.

Tufting and stitching. A strong mattress twine and a long double-pointed mattress needle are required for tufting. The needle is pushed through from the top of the mattress at the marked positions. On the underside it should emerge at the corresponding mark and be re-inserted about $\frac{1}{2}$ in. away, brought to the top and tied with a slip-knot. For the present this is only slightly pulled down and not knotted or tied off, but cut off with 6 in. of twine to spare. Each tie is treated the same way. This will ease the strain on the case ties so that the sewing of the case can be completed. This must be done by hand using a small slip-stitch.

The next item are the two rows of stitching round the sides. These stitches are made with a fine twine and are spaced approximately 2 in. apart. Start with a slip-knot about one-third down the side border and push the needle up through the top of the case, but do not withdraw completely. Return the needle 2 in. along, withdrawing and re-inserting $\frac{1}{4}$ in. away. Continue all round the border like this, the idea being to pull a quantity of stuffing to the edge and retain it in that position.   The mattress is turned over when one edge is finished and the operation is repeated on the other side, thus showing two rows of stitching on the border.   Having finished the

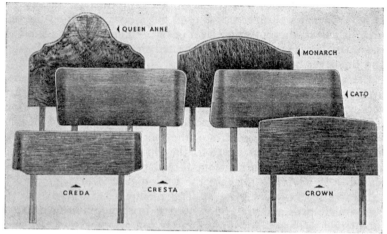

[*Photograph by courtesy Slumberland Ltd., Birmingham.*

VARIETY OF HEADBOARDS FOR DIVAN BEDS.

stitching place the tufts under the twine loops before turning the mattress back again.

The final operation is to place the tufts under the slip-knots, pulling them down and tying off with a knot on the main twine. When tying off the tufts on a spring interior do not pull down as tight as possible, but tight enough only to bring the stuffing to the springing.

18th CENTURY REPRODUCTION CHAIR WITH TAPESTRY COVER.

CHAPTER XXV

UPHOLSTERY REPAIRS

WITH continual use all upholstery becomes shabby and needs renovating. In this and the following chapter we deal with typical operations.

LOOSE SEATS

A loose seat, as its name implies, is made on a frame separate or loose from the main frame, and is used on many different types of chairs and stools.

FIG. I. CHAIR WITH LOOSE SEAT.

The loose seat frame is put together with either tenoned or halved joints. There should be about ⅛ in. clearance all round, and all sharp corners should be removed.

Stripping the old materials. Remove the seat from the chair and place it upside-down on a bench or table. Start to take off the bottom hessian (if any) and the cover by removing the tacks holding these materials in place, using a ripping chisel and mallet, as in Fig. 2. An old screwdriver or chisel can be used as a substitute for the ripping chisel. Drive out the tacks *with* the grain of the wood whenever possible so as to avoid splitting. If the seat is cramped to the bench with a G cramp it makes the work easier. Having cleared the tacks

FIG. 2. KNOCKING OFF OR REMOVING THE OLD COVER.
Note that the ripping chisel or old screwdriver is always worked in
the direction of the grain so that any splitting tendency is avoided.

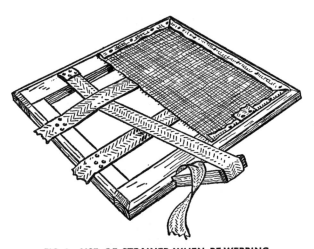

FIG. 3. USE OF STRAINER WHEN RE-WEBBING.
The hessian is tacked on after the webbing is finished. Note that the
edges are double thus obviating any tendency for them to pull through.

on the bottom of the frame turn it over and remove the cover and stuffing. The hessian and webs can then be stripped off in the same way.

Quite often it will be found that plywood has been used as a base for the stuffing. This should be examined to see that it is sound. If it has split it should be discarded, otherwise it may cause squeaking when the chair is used. The nails holding it should be tight, and if necessary fresh nails should be driven in. Glue and cramp any loose joints.

Webbing. The ripping completed, the remaking of the seat is started by fixing fresh webbing. The average size seat requires two strands of web each way, though some larger chairs need three webs. The wide, early Victorian type of chair or a long narrow stool needs a different arrangement—two by three or two by four strands are often necessary. Note the original spacing of the webbing when ripping, and follow the same plan.

The webs are tacked on from the back to the front and from left to right as a general rule. Tack on by turning over the web about 1 in. and using $\frac{5}{8}$-in. improved tacks, spaced as shown in Fig. 3. Stretch to the opposite rail with a web strainer and tack down, leaving 1 in. of web over when cutting off. This is turned over later with the hessian and held down with two tacks. Proceed with the other webs in a similar manner, checking the side ones under and over alternatively before straining.

A piece of hessian is tacked over the webs, starting from the back rail again. Turn over the hessian and tack on with $\frac{1}{2}$-in. or $\frac{5}{8}$-in. improved tacks. Pull as tight as possible to the front rail and tack down through one thickness of hessian, leaving about $\frac{3}{4}$ in. for turning. Repeat this operation from side to side, and finally double over the turnings and the webbing ends.

The stuffing. The stuffing is the next item, but before use it must be carded, or beaten and picked apart so that it is soft and loose, not matted as when removed from the seat. Beating with a stick and pulling apart by hand is the only way unless a carding machine is accessible.

A series of loops of twine are made about 2 in. inwards from the edges of the frame. On a ply base seat these loops would be made by tacking the twine down so as to make two loops on each side. Push a small handful of the stuffing under one of the side or back loops. Pick it over so that it is even and free from lumps. Repeat this operation until the seat is covered with an even layer of stuffing as in Fig. 4.

Cover this layer with an odd piece of material, calico or hessian.

Tack this material in place along the back outer edge with three or four tacks driven partially home, generally called fixing or temporary tacks. Pull over to the front rail, also fixing there from side to side. By releasing the fixing tacks one at a time, and easing down the

FIG. 4. STUFFING PLACED BENEATH LOOPS OF TWINE.
The loops serve to keep the stuffing in position, and thus help to keep the seat in shape.

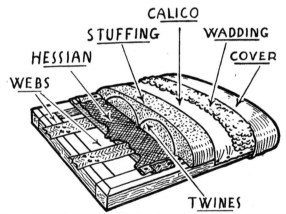

FIG. 5. CUT-AWAY VIEW SHOWING HOW SEAT IS BUILT UP.

material before replacing the tacks, the seat can be gradually moulded into shape. Keep all the stuffing on the top of the seat. Do not allow it to slip over the outer edges, and aim at a nicely rounded contour with the crown, or apex, rather more to the front than to the centre of the seat.

13—P.U.

This completes the stuffing operation unless the actual stuffing is horsehair, or hair as it is usually termed. In the latter case a layer of wadding is placed over the material before pulling over the final cover. The wadding stops the hair from pricking through the cover.

Covering. With the seat already covered with one material the final covering is fairly easy. Start in the same way as with the calico or other material by temporarily fixing all round. This time, however, instead of placing the tacks on the outer edges bring the cover over to the underside of the frame and fix there. If a leathercloth is being used it will probably require several fixings before finally tacking down. The fullness or surplus caused by the rounded shape

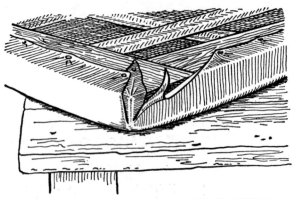

FIG. 6. METHOD OF FOLDING COVER AT CORNER.
The centre is taken straight across and is tacked. A fold is then made at each side.

of the seat needs pulling and easing down until the top is clean and clear of all rucks or folds. A tapestry or soft cover is easier to work into place as there is more stretch or give.

When satisfied that the top is clean finally tack off on the underside with $\frac{3}{8}$-in. or $\frac{1}{2}$-in. fine tacks. Start at the sides, then the front and back, leaving the corners until last. Usually the best method with the corners is to pull the centre of the spare material over the actual point of the corner and make a fold on each side of this point with the remaining surplus material as in Fig. 6. Keep the folds or pleats as tight and small as possible. A piece of hessian neatly turned under at the edges and tacked on to hide the tacks and raw edges of the cover makes a clean finish. This bottom, as it is called, is not a necessity, but finishes the job neatly. Many seats are finished without bottoms, the rough edges and surplus cover being trimmed off neatly with a knife.

CHAPTER XXVI

UPHOLSTERY REPAIRS—*continued*

RE-SEATING AN EASY CHAIR (CUSHION SEAT)

MANY chairs of the type shown in Fig. 1 have given long years of service. They were usually covered with hide or leather-cloth with velveteen cushions. Earlier models had feather-filled

FIG. I. EASY CHAIR TYPICAL OF A PATTERN MADE IN PRE-WAR YEARS.
The seat is usually the first to go, and either the webbing breaks away beneath, or the springs emerge through the top cover.

cushions, whilst later kinds had cushions with spring interiors. Most of these chairs are now in need of renovation.

The seat is usually the first part to need repairs. Sometimes the webbing has broken away and a mess of springs, web, and twine is revealed. Frequently the effects of wear are shown the reverse way. The springs, especially when fixed to metal laths, work through the spring hessian, the stuffing, and finally the cover.

Stripping the seat. In either case it usually means a complete re-seat. A mallet and a ripping chisel or old screwdriver, a knife, and a pair of scissors are required. Knock off the hessian bottom first and if the chair is webbed note how the springs are positioned and how they are sewn to the webs, etc. This may be useful later. Continue the unripping by knocking off the webs and all cover tacked to the bottom rails. Cut out and remove the springs and webs. Turn the chair on to one side and release the tacks, fancy nails, or gimp pins holding the outside arm covering for about 6 in. at each end. It will then be possible to get at the tacks holding the seat cover, scrim, and spring hessian. Release these and repeat the operation on the other outside arm and back.

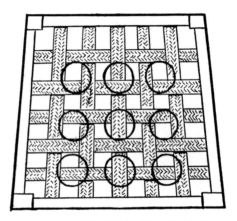

FIG. 2. PLAN SHOWING USUAL SPRING ARRANGEMENT.

The front is the next part to tackle and care must be taken not to damage the cover if it is in good condition and can be used again. If there are covered or polished wood facings on the fronts of the arms these must be carefully eased up to get at the tacks underneath them. They may be nailed, screwed, dowelled, or bolted on.

Webbing and springing. The stripping completed, begin the rebuilding. Start by re-webbing, using good-quality web tacked on with ⅝-in. improved tacks. Five strands of web each way, tightly strained on and checked under and over, are required. If the webs are spaced about 2 in. apart, this should make a good base. Fold the end of the web over about 1 in. and use five tacks at the tacking-on end. Stretch on tightly with a web strainer and tack down with four tacks. Leave 1 in. or so over when cutting off and turn this piece over, tacking it down with two tacks.

If a spring unit on metal laths was used and it is in good condition it can be used again, but this only happens on rare occasions. Some of the springs are generally buckled, thus making the unit useless. From a webbed seat three or four of the springs may be usable. Place these at the back of the new seat and obtain new ones of the same size for the front and middle positions. Sew the springs to the webbing with a strong twine, making three ties to each spring as in Fig. 3. Start with a slip-knot and form a triangle with the three ties. Keep the twine taut when passing from knot to knot.

The top coils of the springs are laced in position with a laid or other strong, non-stretch cord. There is one cord passing over each row of springs from back to front and one from side to side. Knot

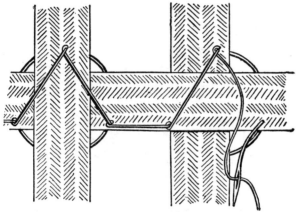

FIG. 3. VIEW FROM BENEATH SHOWING HOW SPRINGS ARE SEWN.

an end of each cord round a tack and fix opposite the centre of each row of springs. Bring the cord up to the second from the top rung of the back spring, making a half-hitch or tie round the coil. Pass to the top coil and tie again, likewise to the top coils of the middle and front springs. Pull the cord tight and tack down on the top seat rail. Repeat over each row, also from side to side rail. The outer side and back springs should lean slightly outwards leaving the centre ones upright when the lacing is completed.

A new, stout piece of hessian will be needed over the springs. This is tacked down all round and the tops of the springs are sewn to it with three ties in a similar manner as when sewing to the webs.

First stuffing. The seat is ready for the first or scrim stuffing. Often with the cheaper grade of work on this type of seat the first stuffing is omitted. Just a thumb roll is tacked along the front seat rail and one layer of stuffing used, then the cover. A more durable seat is obtained by building up with two stuffings. The old stuffing requires carding, or opening out by pulling to pieces. Put it through a carding machine if possible.

Fill in the sides, front, and centre of the seat with stuffing. Cover this with a piece of scrim or light hessian, fixing it in place with temporary tacks. Using a long needle and twine make a square of running-through ties. The ties are made through to the spring hessian and the twine carried along the top of the scrim from tie to tie. Tack the scrim along the front seat rail to form an even edge,

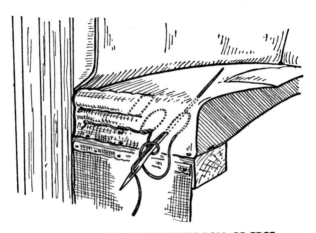

FIG. 4. METHOD OF STITCHING ROLL OR EDGE.

but before doing so try the old cover over it. Probably a new piece of lining or soft material will be required over the platform or centre of the seat, whilst the leathercloth or hide of the front part can be used again. Gauge the height the front edge should finish by trying this cover over the scrim.

Stitching the roll. Finish tacking off the scrim and stitch the roll, or edge. Starting with a blind or sink stitch then a top stitch, as in Fig. 4. Both stitches are started with slip-knots and continued by twisting the twine round the needle as it is withdrawn. With the sink stitch the needle is taken almost through to the top of the scrim before returning, whilst with the top stitch it is taken quite through and returned about ¾ in. back from this point. In most cases this type of chair requires a small roll kept close to the rail. Note the size and height when unripping.

Top stuffing and covering. The top stuffing and covering are the next items. Make a chalk or pencil line across the scrim where the join of the platform material and the front cover should rest. Stretch this seam along the line, fixing it in place with a skewer at each end. Using a half-circular needle and twine sew the seam to the scrim along the line with stitches about 1 in. in length.

Pick a thin layer of top stuffing over the back portion of the seat and pull the platform over. This is fixed in place with a few temporary tacks. The front portion is dealt with in a similar manner and fixed in position. Both portions of the seat are finally eased

FIG. 5. SECTIONAL VIEW SHOWING SPRINGS, STUFFING
AND COVERING.

down and tacked off. This completed, the coverings of the outside arms and back can be retacked into position. Replace carefully the wood facings (if any), also any fancy nails, studs, or mouldings. Turn the chair upside-down and replace the hessian bottom. Unless the old one is in exceptionally good condition use a new piece of hessian.

Finally give any polished parts a good clean, also a rubber of polish if needed. Check the castors, renew if too badly worn, and give a spot of oil to all moving parts.

RE-SEATING A SETTEE (CUSHION-SEAT TYPE)

Start by removing the hessian bottom. To get at this the settee must be turned upside-down. Rest the edge of the seat on a chair or stool.

Ripping the seat. Using a ripping chisel and mallet, knock out the tacks holding the bottom, the webs, and the outside covers. Fig. 7 shows the bottom partly removed. Cut the twines holding the springs to the webs and the spring hessian. Remove the springs and the webs. Release the outside back and arm covers for 6–8 in. from the bottom rails. These may be fixed with antique nails, gimp pins, or studs and banding. The arm facings, which may be finished by any of the above methods or alternatively with polished wood or covered wood facings, may have to be partly removed. This will give

FIG. 6. TYPICAL PRE-WAR SETTEE OF THE TYPE DEALT WITH HERE.
This settee has loose cushions, either feather filled or with spring interiors. The main springing and stuffing of the framework require renewing.

access to the remaining tacks holding the scrim, hessian, and seat cover, which can now be freed by knocking out these tacks. Note the original methods of working as the ripping proceeds.

The webbing, possibly the bottom, and probably the spring hessian can be scrapped as they are generally too worn to be used again. Sort over the springs and discard any with a tendency to buckle. Reject any the slightest degree doubtful, as they will only become worse in use. Cut out the stuffing and put aside to be carded or beaten and picked by hand if a carding machine is not available.

FIG. 7. KNOCKING OUT THE SEAT WITH THE SETTEE UPSIDE-DOWN.
Note method of working as a guide when renewing.

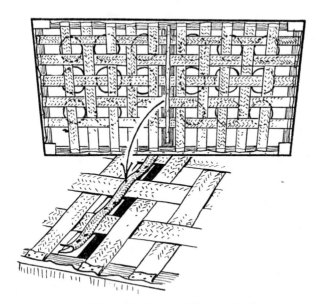

FIG. 8. TYPICAL LAY-OUT OF WEBS AND SPRINGS.
Note the method of supporting the long webs at the centre stretcher rail.

The webbing. Now for the remaking. Before starting to web try all the joints of the frame. If any are loose, knock apart, re-glue, and cramp up tightly. The webbing is started lengthwise by tacking on at the right-hand end looking from the rear. Turn over about 1 in. of web and use five $\frac{5}{8}$-in. improved tacks, or small clout nails if tacks are not obtainable. Stretch tightly with a web strainer to the left-hand rail, tacking down with four tacks. Five is the average number of strands this way, but it varies according to the size of the settee. Trim off the web about 1 in. from the tacks and turn over the end, tacking down with two tacks.

The front to back webs are tacked next, starting from the centre stretcher rail. Place the first web close to this rail, checking it under and over the lengthwise strands of web. Follow up with the remaining webs spaced a trifle under 2 in. apart. An average size settee will probably need five webs on each half of the seat, but don't skimp webbing; use an extra strand or two if in doubt. The strength of a

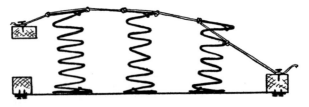

FIG. 9. LACING OF SPRINGS FROM BACK TO FRONT.

webbed seat lies in the interchecking of the strands and the even straining of each web. Stagger the tacks at each end of the web, as this avoids splitting the wood. A piece of web is folded in half and tacked on the centre stretcher rail using two tacks in each space between the lengthwise webs as shown in Fig. 8.

The springing. The springs are the next item. Turn the settee upright and rest it on a pair of trestles. This will be the working position for most of the remaining operations. Eighteen springs are usually required in a seat of this type. Set out in three rows, nine in each half of the seat. The two centre rows (from back to front) are placed close to the stretcher rail. Use the old springs that are in good condition in the back row, keeping the new springs for the positions getting more use. Sew the springs to the webbing with three ties to each spring, starting with a slip-knot.

Having completed the sewing of the bottom of each spring to the web the tops must be dealt with. These are laced in position with a laid cord or good sisal twine. It is generally more convenient to lace from the back to the front first, then from side to side. Cut six lengths of cord and, using $\frac{5}{8}$-in. improved tacks, fix one opposite each row of springs, on the back seat rail. Bring a cord to the second top rung of a back spring, continue to the top rung, as in Fig. 9. Knot or make a hitch around the wire at each point. Carry on in this way across the seat over the top rungs of the middle and front springs, pulling taut and tacking down on the top front rail. Repeat with each row of springs from back to front and likewise from side to side, thus linking all the springs together.

FIG 10. DETAILS OF SCRIM OR FIRST STUFFING.
Also method of sewing cover to the scrim.

The back and two end rows of springs should lean a trifle outwards; also the front row very slightly forward (Fig. 9). The lacing completed, the springs are ready for the spring hessian. A good-quality hessian is pulled over taut and tacked down all round. Do not pull so tight as to loosen the lacing cords.

After the spring hessian is tacked all round the tops of the springs are sewn to it, using a curved spring needle and twine. Use the same method as when sewing to the webs, three ties to each spring.

The first stuffing. A first stuffing covered with a scrim or light hessian makes for a more durable job. Many pre-war suites, particularly the lower priced, cushion-seated variety, omitted this.

A roll or edge was made by tacking a strip of hessian along the front edge and a small quantity of fibre laid on the hessian. The hessian was turned over the fibre and tacked down behind it. A single layer of stuffing was placed on the seat and covered straightway.

To carry on with the first stuffing proper cut a piece of scrim or hessian the size of the seat, allowing for the build-up of the edge. Temporarily fix this with about six tacks along the top of the back seat rail. The scrim is laid aside over the back whilst stuffing. Fill up the spaces between the arms and the seat, and the back and the seat with fibre. Make three or four loops of twine along the front edge and pick an even quantity of fibre under these loops. Finally spread a thin layer of stuffing over the centre of the seat.

Bring the scrim over the whole and fix it on the front edge of the front rail. Using a 10- or 12-in. double-pointed straight needle and twine, make a series of ties and running stitches commonly termed running-through. The idea is to keep the stuffing in place by binding it between the scrim and spring hessian. Do not finally tie off until the scrim is all tacked and the edge completed.

The next operation is to tack down evenly the front edge or roll. Loosen the fixing tacks one at a time and pick over the edge stuffing, adding extra if needed, until a firm, even edge is obtained. Tack this down with $\frac{3}{8}$- or $\frac{1}{2}$-in. improved tacks about 1 in. apart. It is advisable to try the cover over the scrim stuffing before completing the tacking off as it will help to ensure the correct height being obtained.

Two rows of stitching are required to bring the roll into shape, a sink or blind stitch, and a top stitch as in Fig. 10. The blind stitch is made first, close to the tacks. Its object is to bring the stuffing forward ready for the next stitch to form into a firm edge. The edge formed by the top stitch should be about the size of the forefinger. Both stitches commence with slip-knots and continue with ties made by twisting the twine round the needle as it is returned about $\frac{3}{4}$ in. behind the point of insertion. With the blind stitch the needle is returned before the eye reaches the scrim on the top of the seat. The top stitch goes quite through and takes up about 1 in. of scrim before it is returned.

Replacing the cover. Replacing the covering of the seat is the next item. On a cushion-seated job more often than not this cover consists of two pieces of different material sewn together, the front seat piece being hide or leathercloth and the rear portion, commonly called the platform, a soft material. Check both materials to see if sound and usable, also that all seams are tight and strong. A line is drawn on the scrim at the point where the front material and platform meet. The seam of these two materials is sewn to the scrim along this line with a thin twine.

A quite thin layer of stuffing is picked on the platform part of the seat and the cover drawn over. The smaller, front portion is covered with a firmer filling of stuffing, the covering pulled over and temporarily tacked. Each section of the seat is eased down and finally tacked off. The outside arms and back are replaced in their respective positions; also the front facings. When these are all tacked in place the bottom is covered with hessian, either a new piece or the old piece if still serviceable.

The cushions. The cushions when feather filled may require new inside cases of downproof calico if the feathers are working through. Otherwise a good beating and banging to loosen the feathers and clear the dust will help to revive them. The spring interior types are a more difficult proposition. If the springs are displaced it generally means replacing with a new spring interior unit. Occasionally the old one can be taken out and reversed if the back springs of the unit are in good condition. In either case the stuffing will need rearranging over the springs and probably require a fresh layer of linter's felt.

Alternatively scrap the old cushions and replace with foamed latex or polyether units. Make up new cases in a modern fabric to tone with the older chair and settee coverings.

Cut paper templates of the seat sizes and obtain the nearest foam units to these sizes. Use the templates to cut the cushion tops and bottoms. Make the borders the thickness of the units plus the sewing allowances but only just the size so they are a tight fit which will give a clean, neat cushion.

INDEX